Your Hyperactive Child

Your Hyperactive Child

A Parent's Guide to Coping with Attention Deficit Disorder

BARBARA INGERSOLL

Foreword by Judith L. Rapoport, M.D.,
and Alan J. Zametkin, M.D.
NATIONAL INSTITUTE OF MENTAL HEALTH

MAIN
STREET
BOOKS

NEW YORK   LONDON   TORONTO   SYDNEY   AUCKLAND

A MAIN STREET BOOK

PUBLISHED BY DOUBLEDAY
a division of Bantam Doubleday Dell Publishing Group, Inc.
666 Fifth Avenue, New York, New York 10103

MAIN STREET BOOKS, DOUBLEDAY, and the portrayal of a
building with a tree are trademarks of Doubleday, a
division of Bantam Doubleday Dell Publishing Group, Inc.

Library of Congress Cataloging-in-Publication Data
Ingersoll, Barbara D., 1945–
    Your hyperactive child: a parent's guide to coping
        with attention deficit disorder / Barbara Ingersoll;
    foreword by Judith L. Rapoport and Alan J. Zametkin.—1st ed.
        p.   cm.
    Bibliography: p.
    Includes index.
    ISBN 0-385-24069-4
    ISBN 0-385-24070-8 (paperbound)

    1. Attention deficit disorders.   2. Hyperactive child syndrome.
I. title.
RJ496.A86I54   1988   87-36535
618.92'8589—dc19   CIP

With appreciation and affection
to John F. Kelley, M.D.,
scholar, teacher, friend

Contents

List of Figures

Foreword

For three decades, psychiatry has been in the process of a revolutionary change. Major changes have taken place in the way we think about psychiatric disorders, the way we study them, and the way we treat them.

Psychiatry has turned, for example, from emphasis on disturbances in the *mind* to a search for disturbances in the *brain* as the source of disordered behavior and emotions. Research in the neurosciences has produced enormous gains in our understanding of how the brain works and how breakdowns in the brain affect the way we think, feel, and behave. Carefully controlled scientific investigation has replaced "armchair theorizing" as the principal means of advancing our knowledge about what causes psychiatric disorders and what treatment approaches are likely to be most helpful.

For some time, research efforts were directed primarily toward adult psychiatric disorders, with child psychiatry lagging behind. Recently, however, there has been an explosion of scientific interest in child psychiatry. Much of this exciting research has been done in the area of Attention-deficit Hyperactivity Disorder (ADHD), providing us with important new insights into the causes of the disorder, its course, and how it can be most effectively treated.

It is unfortunate that so little of this valuable information has been made readily available to parents, teachers, and others most intimately involved in the lives of ADHD children. Confused by myths and misinformation, these "front line" people often do not know where to turn for reliable information and appropriate help.

In one volume, Barbara Ingersoll has nicely summarized the state of the art in the field of ADHD. It provides parents, teachers, and clinicians the latest information on a field that is extremely difficult to review, given the increase in information that has been generated by excellent and well-controlled research in this area. A great service of this work is that it treats the subject with a well-rounded approach, ignoring neither the biological, the psychological, or the social aspects of the problem.

In a style that is readable, entertaining, and informative, Barbara Ingersoll draws from her vast clinical experience with these children and their families. She clearly, concisely, and factually delivers to the reader a work that, for years to come, will be a great aid to any one who comes in contact with children with this spectrum of disorders.

JUDITH L. RAPOPORT, M.D.
Chief, Child Psychiatry Branch

ALAN J. ZAMETKIN, M.D.
Child Psychiatry Branch
National Institute of Mental Health

Author's Note

The American Psychiatric Association has officially adopted the term "Attention-deficit Hyperactivity Disorder" to describe the condition we used to call simply "hyperactivity." Although the new term more accurately describes the condition, it is also rather unwieldy. For this reason, I have used the more familiar term "hyperactive" throughout most of this book to describe children who have Attention-deficit Hyperactivity Disorder. The shorter term "Attention Deficit Disorder" is also commonly used by clinicians and families to refer to this disorder.

Your Hyperactive Child

1

What Is Attention-deficit Hyperactivity Disorder?

The young mother in the pediatrician's office appeared on the verge of tears. As she looked from the doctor to her four-year-old son, her voice quavered. "Doctor, I know I shouldn't say this in front of him, but this child is driving me crazy! He's on the go night and day. If I take my eyes off of him for a minute he tears the house apart. He has to have his own way, or he throws himself on the floor and screams. Every time I take him anywhere, it's a disaster. He just goes wild. And I can't leave him with a sitter—I can't find anyone who's willing to watch him because he's such a handful. Nursery school didn't work, either: he lasted two weeks. Have you ever known anyone who was expelled from *nursery school?*" She tried to smile but managed only a grimace. "My husband says that I'm the problem: he thinks I'm too lenient with him. But my mother says he's just 'all boy' and needs to let off steam. I don't know—maybe he's 'hyper.' All I know is, we've got to do something because I just can't take it anymore."

The psychologist greeted seven-year-old Robin and her parents and ushered them into the office. Although Robin seemed very much at ease as she wandered around the room examining various objects, her parents looked distinctly uncomfortable. Each looked to the other to begin, then both began speaking at once.

"Doctor, we've been having a problem with . . ."

"We're here because Robin's teacher . . ."

Both stopped. With a nervous laugh, Robin's mother continued. "Robin's teacher thought we should see someone—I mean, thought we should see you—because Robin just isn't settling down in second grade. Her first-grade teacher had some problems with her, too, but we thought she just needed a little time to mature."

Robin's father broke in to explain. "We know she's bright: she was reading when she was in kindergarten. But the teacher says she never finishes her work. She spends all of her time wandering around the classroom or gazing off into space."

"Or annoying the other children," Robin's mother interrupted. "The teacher has moved her desk three times. Now she's sitting right under the teacher's nose, but it hasn't solved the problem." She paused, then went on. "You know, when she was in kindergarten, one of the teachers mentioned hyperactivity. We never gave it much thought because she can sit for hours in front of the TV or playing with puzzles. But now I'm beginning to wonder . . . Doctor, do you think she might be hyperactive?"

What is hyperactivity? How can you tell if your child is hyperactive? Myths and misconceptions about hyperactivity abound, and it is probably safe to say that few people outside the mental health professions really understand the term. Even professionals disagree, although hyperactivity is the most common childhood psychiatric disorder and accounts for at least half of all referrals to child mental health clinics.

The confusion has been compounded by the bewildering variety of terms used over the years to describe the condition —terms such as "minimal brain damage" or "minimal brain dysfunction" (often called simply MBD), "hyperkinesis," "hyperkinetic reaction," and "hyperactivity." These changes in terms reflect changes in thinking about the nature of the disorder itself. Thus, the term "minimal brain damage" gave way to the labels "hyperkinetic" and "hyperactive," which were replaced, in turn, by the term "Attention Deficit Disorder" and, most recently, Attention-deficit Hyperactivity Disorder (ADHD).

Early in the century, descriptions appeared of children who were excessively active and distractible, impulsive, unruly, and difficult to manage at home and in school. Although some of these children were of normal intelligence, with no detectable brain injury or disease, other children's symptoms were associated with known brain damage or disease. The suspected link between brain damage and hyperactive behavior was strengthened by the 1918 encephalitis epidemic, when doctors observed that many children developed this behavior pattern following recovery from encephalitis.

Animal research and studies of children with epilepsy and other central nervous system disorders seemed to support the link between brain damage and hyperactive behavior. To explain those cases in which the behavior pattern appeared in the absence of known brain damage, psychologists came up with the terms "minimal brain damage" or "minimal brain dysfunction"; that is, these children were thought to be suffering from brain damage that could not be detected by available medical tests. These terms were in widespread use in the fifties. Experts in the field recommended classrooms with very little stimulation as helpful environments for these children, and the prevailing belief was that they would outgrow their problems by adolescence.

As early as 1937, doctors reported that stimulant medication helped hyperactive children. For years, however, these reports aroused little interest. The drug revolution in psychiatry in the 1950s generated renewed interest in stimulant medication, and, by the mid-sixties, stimulants were widely used in the treatment of hyperactivity. This period also saw an upsurge of research into the nature and treatment of the disorder itself. The term "MBD" came under fire because, researchers argued, it was not certain that these children were brain-damaged: brain damage had been inferred only from behavioral signs. Scientists saw excessive motor activity, which brought the child into conflict with his environment, as the core problem in the disorder, and they devised ingenious devices to measure and study motor activity levels. With emphasis on motor activity, the terms "hyperkinesis" ("excessive motion") and "hyperactivity" came to be substituted for MBD. In the second edition of the American Psychiatric Association's *Diagnostic and Statistical Manual,* published in 1968, the condition was labeled "hyperkinetic reaction of childhood."

By the early 1970s, however, the focus began to move away from motor activity. Led by the pioneering work of psychologist Virginia Douglas at McGill University, scientists turned to the study of attention span problems in hyperactive children. According to Douglas, it is not really excessive activity that brings the child into conflict with others; rather, the problem lies in his short attention span, his impulsiveness, and his inability to "stop, look, and listen" before taking action. Unable to pause and think through the consequences of his actions, the child careens or wanders through life, responding impulsively to whatever happens to catch his attention at the moment.

This new focus on attention and impulsiveness has resulted in yet another change in terminology. In the most recent edition of the American Psychiatric Association's diagnostic handbook, the disorder is called *Attention-deficit Hyperactivity Disorder.* This label reflects the fact that attentional problems are very prominent among children previously labeled simply "hyperactive." It reminds us, too, that some children who are not at all hyperactive or disruptive can have severe difficulties with attention and concentration. Since their symptoms are less obvious and less troublesome to adults, these children were often not referred for help in the past. We now know, however, that their problems—social, academic, and emotional—are as serious as those of the more classically hyperactive child.

DIAGNOSTIC GUIDELINES

How can we tell the difference between a youngster who is normally bouncy and exuberant and one who is truly hyperactive? Does every child who daydreams in class have ADHD? Guidelines for diagnosing ADHD are outlined in the *Diagnostic and Statistical Manual,* published by the American Psychiatric Association (Third Edition, Revised, 1987). This manual represents an attempt to standardize diagnostic practices among psychiatrists, psychologists, and others who diagnose psychiatric disorders. The guidelines are helpful because they provide a common language for mental health professionals engaged in research and clinical practice.

The *Diagnostic and Statistical Manual* provides the following guidelines for diagnosing Attention-deficit Hyperactivity Disorder.

A. A disturbance of six months or more, during which at least *eight* of the following behaviors are present:
   1. Often fidgets with hands or feet or squirms in seat (in adolescents, may be limited to subjective feelings of restlessness)
   2. Has difficulty remaining seated when required to
   3. Is easily distracted by extraneous stimuli
   4. Has difficulty awaiting turn in games or group situations

5. Often blurts out answers to questions before they have been completed

6. Has difficulty following through on instructions from others (not due to oppositional behavior or failure of comprehension); for example, fails to finish chores

7. Has difficulty sustaining attention in tasks or play activities

8. Often shifts from one uncompleted activity to another

9. Has difficulty playing quietly

10. Often talks excessively

11. Often interrupts or intrudes on others; for example, butts into other children's games

12. Often doesn't seem to listen to what is being said to him or her

13. Often loses things necessary for tasks or activities at school or at home (for example, toys, pencils, books, assignments)

14. Often engages in physically dangerous activities without considering possible consequences (not for the purpose of thrill seeking); for example, runs into street without looking

B. Onset before the age of seven

Although most professionals agree that these guidelines are very helpful, some have noted important oversights. Psychologist Russell Barkley, an authority on ADHD, is among the critics. Dr. Barkley points out that impulsiveness, hyperactivity, and attentional problems are not the only major symptoms in many hyperactive children. His research, for example, demonstrates that these children very often have problems with social conduct. Although they know the rules, they seem to lack the self-control to follow them. They also tend to be more negative and attention-seeking and in greater need of supervision than other children. Therefore, Dr. Barkley argues, *difficulty following rules* should also be considered a major feature of the disorder.

Likewise, my own experience with hyperative children strongly suggests that, no matter how hard they try, many of these children simply cannot abide by the same rules that other children follow. My experience also indicates that negativism, disobedience, and a general attitude of "I-don't-wanna-and-I'm-not-gonna!" are common features of the disorder. Certainly, not all hyperactive children are negative and disobedient: many have sweet dispositions and seem to try very hard to please. However, a large number are described as very stubborn, not able to tolerate being thwarted, and quite insistent on having their own way at any cost. Why these features should characterize so many hyperactive children is not known at this time.

HOW WIDESPREAD IS THE PROBLEM?

Because definitions of the disorder have varied, so have estimates of its occurrence. Until recently, most experts agreed that approximately 3–5 percent of school-age children could be diagnosed as hyperactive. They also agreed that ADHD is about six times more common among boys than among girls.

New research, however, suggests that these figures may be seriously misleading because they do not include children (especially girls) whose problems are attentional rather than behavioral. Led by the husband wife team of Doctors Bennett and Sally Shaywitz,[1] researchers at the Yale Child Study Center compared hyperactive girls with hyperactive boys. They found that girls with ADHD had more serious problems with complex thinking and language, while hyperactive boys were more overactive, aggressive, and disruptive. Hyperactive girls were also more likely than boys to be rejected by other children.

Since the problems of hyperactive girls are not as visible or as troublesome to adults as the problems of hyperactive boys,

girls are less likely to come to professional attention. Therefore, they are probably not accurately reflected in the statistics
on ADHD. In fact, according to the Yale group, our current
figures on ADHD may be just the tip of a much larger iceberg.

THROUGH THE YEARS: THE HYPERACTIVE CHILD FROM INFANCY TO ADULTHOOD

INFANCY

As many as 60–70 percent of hyperactive children show
specific, telltale symptoms by two years of age or even earlier.
In fact, many of these children seem to "get off on the wrong
foot" in life from the first days and weeks. They are inclined to
be somewhat irregular and unpredictable in biological habits
such as eating, sleeping, and elimination, so that planning a
routine around them is difficult. Sleep, especially, is irregular,
and many seem to need less sleep than the average infant. It is
not unusual for parents to report being awakened by crying
several times in the course of a night during the first two or
more years of the child's life.

The mood of the hyperactive infant is generally negative;
these infants are likely to cry and fuss more than they gurgle
and coo. They adjust very slowly to change and often respond
negatively to anything new.

As we might expect, parents often report high levels of
activity, and some mothers of hyperactive children describe
excessive activity even before birth, such as, "He kicked so
hard that I was sure he'd break my ribs" or "I knew he was
going to be a handful before he was even born: he didn't give
me a moment's peace for nine months." Hyperactive infants
are often restless and difficult to hold, so feeding such an
infant or changing his diaper can become a real struggle. It is
not uncommon for parents to complain of crib mattresses
(and even cribs) being demolished by kicking, bouncing, and
rocking. Many youngsters become accomplished "escape art-

ists" quite early, and parents may have to go to extreme lengths to keep the child from climbing out of his crib in the middle of the night. "I feel awful seeing my child in a cage," sighed one father who escape-proofed his son's crib with chicken wire. "But it's better than having him break his neck falling out of the crib."

Of course, not every active, fussy baby or poor sleeper turns out to be a hyperactive child, nor does every hyperactive youngster have such a stormy infancy. In looking back, you may even remember your child's early years as a calm, pleasant period. Chances are, however, that you can recall early and repeated bouts of sickness, since health problems so often complicate the hyperactive child's first years. Recent research, in fact, highlights health problems in infancy as particularly important indicators of risk for ADHD. Allergies are common, and these children seem especially prone to colds, asthma, and upper respiratory infections. There are also indications that serous otitis media (an ear infection with a buildup of fluid in the middle ear) is particularly common in hyperactive infants.

After a pregnancy complicated by toxemia, Ryan was born mildly jaundiced. There were early feeding problems: Ryan nursed poorly and often vomited after a feeding. He also suffered from diarrhea. The pediatrician suspected a milk allergy, and several alternative formulas were tried, but with only limited success. From the age of about six months he suffered repeated ear infections. According to his exhausted parents, Ryan "slept very little and cried a lot." Desperate, they took turns walking the floor with him, even driving him around the neighborhood in the middle of the night in the hope that the ride would lull him to sleep—or at least quiet his screams.

To listen to Sharon's parents describe her, "She was born kicking and screaming, and she hasn't stopped since!" Having raised two other youngsters with no more than the average amount of difficulty, they anticipated her birth with confidence in their own parenting abilities. However, Sharon soon shattered their composure. Unlike her siblings, Sharon did not settle into a routine at home. In fact, her mother says, "Nothing about her has *ever* been routine." Any noise or light seemed to startle her out of all proportion to its intensity and provoked lengthy episodes of loud crying. Her parents could do little to console her: she did not seem to enjoy being cuddled, and efforts to comfort her were usually futile. Generally irritable and unsmiling, she was not very responsive to smiles or other attempts at social interaction, and the other children soon gave up trying to play with their baby sister. Sharon's mother says, "I don't blame them for avoiding her—there are certainly times when I wish I could do the same."

THE PRESCHOOL YEARS

High levels of activity continue to characterize the hyperactive child during the preschool years. As many parents have observed, "He never walks—he runs." An additional complication is the fact that, although some hyperactive children have good gross motor development, many more (probably about half) are awkward and clumsy. The combination of clumsiness, high activity level, and fearlessness so often seen in these youngsters forces parents to provide almost constant supervision lest the child endanger himself. Unfortunately, some of these children seem drawn to danger like a magnet, and many parents recount tales of two-year-olds who entertain themselves by turning on stoves, inserting objects into electrical outlets, and climbing out third-floor windows to the roof.

Even parents who do not have to contend with constant running, bouncing, and jumping comment that the child is "into everything." A common complaint is, "I can't leave him alone for a single minute. If I turn my back, he's doing something he shouldn't be doing." Noted authority Dr. Paul Wender gives this colorful summary: "Parents frequently report that after an active and restless infancy, the child stood and walked at an early age, and then, like an infant King Kong, burst the bars of his crib and marched forth to destroy the house."[2]

Despite the best efforts of parents to childproof the house, property damage and harm to the child occur frequently. Accidental poisoning, for example, is much more common among hyperactive children than among other children, and it has been estimated that one boy out of four who is treated for accidental poisoning during the preschool years is hyperactive. Hyperactive children are also at least three times as likely as other children to have experienced four or more serious accidents during childhood.

Parents often notice that the hyperactive preschooler has a very short attention span. At the same time, if the child is doing something of interest to him, it can be almost impossible to distract him or divert his attention. These children do seem unusually strong-willed and unresponsive to discipline. Many are prone to fits of temper that in frequency, duration, and intensity exceed the occasional tantrums of the average preschooler. Not all parents describe what we usually think of as "temper tantrums": many describe a child who cannot tolerate any type of frustration and simply "falls apart" when things are not as he wishes them to be.

Taking a hyperactive youngster out in public can be exhausting and embarrassing. Even older hyperactive children often seem compelled to touch and handle everything they see. Impulsiveness is a problem, too, and desperate parents may resort to using a harness to keep the child from darting away in stores and busy streets. Unfortunately, this practice often brings scowls and disapproving comments from total strangers, so the parents cannot win either way!

Toilet training is frequently a struggle with the hyperactive preschooler, and many are not bowel-trained until after the age of three. (In fact, it is not uncommon to find the hyperactive child still having bowel and bladder accidents up to several years beyond the age at which most children are completely trained.) The youngster may be delayed in other areas, too, such as fine motor coordination. Thus, even a bright hyperactive child may not be able to participate successfully in preschool cut-and-paste activities, and he may require help with dressing and eating when other children his age have become largely self-reliant. Delays in talking and speech problems are also more common among hyperactive children.

In a play group or preschool setting the hyperactive child's problems may become glaringly apparent, especially if the child is aggressive and destructive. The more structured the setting, the more apt the child is to come into conflict with peers, teachers, and others.

By the time Joshua was four years old, his weary parents felt as if they were living in a combat zone. His mother, who described him as a "demolition expert," recounted tales of freshly painted walls "repainted" with butter, dollar bills taken from her purse and tossed from a balcony to the street below, and "acres" of torn curtains, shattered toys, and battered furniture. Although Josh could be affectionate and charming, he was given to unpredictable outbursts of anger during which he was aggressive and destructive. In any setting, he demanded to be the center of attention, and his boisterous, show-off behavior was deeply embarrassing to his parents when guests were present in the home. An attempt to enroll him in a play group at age three ended in failure when he repeatedly reduced the other three-year-olds to tears by hitting, shoving, and grabbing toys. Most recently, he had been asked to leave an expressive dance class for preschoolers because he could not follow directions and was "too boisterous and disruptive."

MIDDLE CHILDHOOD

The hyperactive child's problems continue through the elementary school years. Indeed, school presents the child with greater demands for self-control, and even the child who was able to "squeak by" in the less structured settings of home and preschool may fail miserably when confronted with these demands. Tolerant parents who considered their child to be merely "all boy" or "lively and exuberant" are apt to be unpleasantly surprised to receive an urgent request for a parent-teacher conference to discuss their child's problems. Compared to kindergarten, first grade places much greater emphasis on following instructions, working independently, and abiding by classroom rules. The hyperactive child, with his restlessness and short attention span, is quickly labeled "immature." This view is bolstered by the fact that the hyperactive child is often disorganized, forgetful, and messy—qualities not highly prized by most teachers. The hyperactive child has a tendency to blurt things out in class, demand immediate teacher attention when he has a question, and not to wait his turn in the classroom and on the playground. In a typical class of twenty-five to thirty children, this kind of disruptive behavior can strain a teacher's patience to the breaking point. If the child has emotional outbursts in reaction to even minor events, the teacher may begin to suspect that the child is seriously emotionally disturbed. This is especially likely if the child daydreams a great deal and spends much of his time in class drawing pictures of weapons, monsters, and other themes that suggest a bizarre fantasy life.

Learning problems, quite common among hyperactive children, further complicate the child's difficulties in school. Because the child's performance varies from week to week and even day to day, teachers may assume that the child is simply lazy and could do the work "if he really wanted to."

Problems in school spill over into the home, adding tension and discord. Pitched battles over homework occur daily. Mornings are chaotic as parents try to coax, cajole, and coerce their "morning dawdlers" into some semblance of order by the time the school bus arrives. Weekends are filled with arguments about household chores and other unmet responsibilities. In all of these situations, the child's inability to tolerate frustration and his "low boiling point" increase the likelihood that confrontations will lead to tears, shrieks, and tantrums.

These qualities also pose problems with friends and playmates. Because he cannot tolerate the frustration of losing a game, the hyperactive child often erupts in angry outbursts, sometimes accompanied by verbal or physical aggression. Hyperactive children can be so single-minded in pursuit of what they want that they tend to be blind to the feelings of others. Thus, they are often bossy with peers. They tend to play with younger children, who allow them to dominate, or sometimes with older children, who may be more tolerant of their behavior.

The hyperactive child who is clumsy has an additional social handicap during the elementary school years. At a time when other children are particularly interested in team sports, the hyperactive child is often last to be chosen when teams are formed on the playground and in physical education class.

Rejected by peers, unsuccessful in school, and frequently in trouble with parents and other authority figures—it is no wonder that many develop a poor self-image by late childhood. Although they may blame others for their difficulties and show maddeningly little insight into the role their own behavior plays in their problems, many hyperactive children secretly believe that they are stupid, unlovable, and worthless. It is not surprising that many turn to negative ways of gaining attention: bragging, fighting, lying, and stealing can become chronic problems.

As a preschooler, Eric showed little interest in such activities as coloring and learning letters. His concerned mother, herself a teacher, sought out a private school that boasted small classes and individualized attention. It soon became apparent, however, that this was not enough. Although Eric's teachers considered him a bright, friendly little boy, they found his high spirits and boundless energy difficult to manage in the classroom. His restlessness and need for constant physical contact with others led the other children to view him as a nuisance and he soon gained a reputation on the playground as a crybaby. He also had academic difficulties, despite high scores on an individually administered intelligence test. His parents and teachers hoped that repeating first grade would give him a chance to mature a bit, but these hopes were dashed very early in the new school year when Eric's old problems continued without improvement. Eric himself was keenly aware of his difficulties and, on one occasion, inquired wistfully whether brain surgery might help him "be a better kid."

Jamie's embittered mother described her nine-year-old son as "a bum—just like his father." His parents had divorced when Jamie was six. His alcoholic father was erratic with visits and child support and soon disappeared from the picture. When Jamie had serious behavior problems in the first grade, the school psychologist attributed his belligerence, aggression, and frequent tantrums to the effects of a broken home. She described him as "an angry, frightened child who fears being overwhelmed by his own aggressive impulses." She also thought that his academic difficulties stemmed from his emotional concerns and recommended psychotherapy. During two years of individual psychotherapy, however, his behavior failed to improve. In school, he was placed in a class for emotionally disturbed children, where he continued to challenge all authority. In the neighborhood, he was known as a thief and a bully. His mother admitted that she was unable to control him and was open in expressing her anger and frustration. She was particularly disgusted by the fact that, at age nine, he continued to wet the bed almost nightly and still occasionally soiled his pants.

ADOLESCENCE

Previously it was thought that hyperactive children would improve markedly in adolescence, and parents were often reassured, "Don't worry; he'll outgrow it." Certainly, children tend to calm down with age: we need only compare the general levels of activity on an elementary school playground and the grounds of a high school to see that this is true for all children, not just those who are hyperactive. However, while decreases in extremely high levels of activity may make the hyperactive teenager less conspicuous in a group, this does not eliminate his behavioral and emotional problems and learning difficulties.

Only a minority of hyperactive children—perhaps 20 percent or so—are symptom-free by adolescence. Earlier optimism has waned in the face of new evidence indicating that the majority of hyperactive children continue to have significant problems as adolescents. In fact, many experts believe that the teenage years are even more difficult than earlier periods because the hyperactive child's problems are now complicated by all the stresses and difficulties of normal adolescence.

School performance, in particular, is apt to be a problem for the hyperactive adolescent. In the laboratory, tests such as the Matching Familiar Figures Test reveal continued weaknesses in attention and impulse control. These weaknesses show up in poor scholastic performance, and, despite normal or even superior intelligence, the hyperactive adolescent is often a chronic underachiever. School failure is common. By adolescence, as many as half have failed at least one grade in school and about one third have repeated two or more grades. The "battle of the homework," begun years earlier, escalates as college admission looms closer. High school teachers are reluctant to continue programs such as daily notes home, which helped to keep the youngster on track in elementary school. "He's old enough to take some responsibility for himself," they point out.

Parents, too—weary after years of nagging the child about homework and chores—believe that the teenager should be capable of assuming greater responsibility. The rebelliousness, argumentativeness, and moodiness of normal adolescence may be exaggerated in the hyperactive adolescent, so it is likely that there will be frequent conflict between parent and child. Many parents both long for and dread the day the child will leave the parental home. "How can he possibly survive on his own?" they ask. "He can't even remember to take a shower unless I'm after him all the time!"

Other, more serious worries confront the parents of some hyperactive teenagers whose chronic problems with rules bring them into conflict with law enforcement agencies. "I used to worry that he wouldn't get into college," one mother sighed. "Now I just pray that he stays out of jail." Researchers disagree on exact figures, but a significant number of hyperactive youngsters develop patterns of serious antisocial behavior during adolescence. The risk seems greatest for those who continue to have two or more symptoms of the syndrome during late adolescence. Among this group the chances of serious antisocial behavior and drug or alcohol abuse are estimated to be as high as 50 percent.

Adolescence is a time when the young person prepares for the transition to life on his own. During this transitional period, friends serve as a bridge between dependence on the family and adult independence. For this reason, the peer group assumes great importance in the teenager's daily life. Unfortunately, many hyperactive teenagers are not well liked or accepted by other teenagers. Because they are often impulsive, immature, and poor achievers in the classroom and on the athletic field, many hyperactive teenagers are shunned by their age-mates, who view them as loud, silly, and "weird."

As we might expect, the self-image of the hyperactive adolescent reflects his many failures at home, in school, and in the community. Their self-esteem is often low, and, when asked to describe themselves, they frequently describe what they are *not:* "I'm not too great in school"; "I'm not real popular"; "I'm not as smart as my brother." In comparison with other adolescents, hyperactive teenagers are more often depressed. Some doctors and researchers have speculated that demoralization and depression result from continually being at odds with parents, peers, and others. However, others have suggested that sadness, demoralization, and depressed mood may simply be another characteristic feature of the disorder itself.

Sixteen-year-old Cary was referred for a psychological evaluation because, despite average intelligence, he was failing all of his major subjects in school. At sixteen, he was still in the ninth grade, having repeated the second and seventh grades. Cary had been evaluated by a psychologist in the third grade. The diagnosis was ADHD, and a recommendation was made for medication, which seemed to help by reducing excessive activity. The psychologist also recommended special education, but Cary's parents and teachers continued to view him as simply "unmotivated," so little remedial assistance was provided.

Homework, a problem since the elementary school years, was a source of constant conflict between Cary and his parents. This contributed to the already high levels of tension in the home. Cary's father had also been a hyperactive child and continued to show many symptoms of the disorder, including an explosive temper and extreme restlessness. In addition, Cary's mother had been on antidepressant medication for several years following a suicide attempt.

Cary's parents mentioned a couple of encounters with the police. Although the offenses were relatively minor—setting a brush fire at the age of eight and two incidents of vandalism—they were sufficient to give Cary a juvenile record. His parents also were concerned about Cary's lack of friends. "He's always been too much of a loner, and I don't think that's good," his mother said.

At first, Cary was quite defensive and reluctant to talk about his difficulties. Other than stating, "I hate school and I *hate* homework," he denied any problems in his life. However, he scored in the moderately depressed range on a depression inventory, and his responses indicated feelings of failure and hopelessness. When the interviewer observed, "You feel pretty low about yourself," he finally admitted, "I feel lower than low. I feel like I'm just dirt under somebody's feet."

THE ADULT YEARS

The major symptoms of ADHD appear to decrease in intensity with increasing age, but many adults who were previously diagnosed as hyperactive continue to have problems with attention and concentration. These difficulties tend to be most noticeable when the individual must deal with tasks that are not particularly interesting or enjoyable. Poor organization, absentmindedness, and forgetfulness often annoy spouses and employers and complicate the lives of hyperactive adults.

Although he no longer runs through the halls or bounces on the furniture, the hyperactive adult may still be more restless and fidgety than those around him. Many find it difficult to sit down and relax, noting "I can't just sit—I've got to be doing something." This restlessness can be disturbing to others: one patient reported that his inability to sit still "makes my roommate crazy." The wife of another patient complained that she could not rely on her husband to babysit their young children because "If he's cooped up in the house for a couple of hours, he can't stand it. He's like a caged lion." On the positive side, some hyperactive adults channel excess energy into such productive activities as home improvement projects, overtime on the job, and even additional part-time employment. In fact, many hyperactive adults tend to "find themselves" after years of being considered misfits, when they enter a career that interests and challenges them.

The emotional highs and lows of childhood and adolescence may continue into the adult years. Unfortunately, however, the highs gradually tend to disappear, while the lows persist. Mood problems appear to be quite common: as many as three quarters of hyperactive adults complain of frequent low or depressed moods. Many also report chronic pessimism and inability to really enjoy life and describe themselves as tense and "hassled." Poor frustration tolerance is common, and there is a tendency to overreact to the normal ups and downs of daily life. Irritability and hot temper may also persist. When this is the case, the individual's personal life may suffer as friends and family grow weary and resentful of repeated angry outbursts. In severe cases, child abuse or assault charges may result from poor temper control.

Statistics concerning outcomes in adult years are confusing. Studies which have followed hyperactive children into adulthood have focused on widely differing groups, so vastly different results have been reported by different researchers. Some studies, for example, have indicated higher rates of drug and alcohol abuse among hyperactive adults, while others have not found this to be the case. However, there seems to be general agreement on the following points:

• Among hyperactive individuals, about half "outgrow" the syndrome by the early adult years, while half continue to have mildly to severely disabling symptoms. As mentioned, individuals who continue to have two or more symptoms of the syndrome are most likely to engage in serious antisocial behavior and/or drug or alcohol abuse during adult years.

• There is no evidence that a childhood diagnosis of ADHD increases the risk of a psychotic disorder (a severe type of mental disorder characterized by hallucinations, delusions, disordered thinking, and bizarre behavior). Compared to the general population, however, hyperactive adults are at greater risk for psychiatric hospitalization and psychiatric disorders, especially "personality disorders," which are characterized by dependency, immaturity, and impulsiveness.

• As adults, many hyperactive individuals continue to have low self-esteem. Many, too, describe their childhoods as unhappy.

• Many hyperactive adults appear to make a better overall adjustment once they leave school. Freed from a setting which emphasizes their weaknesses and faced with more options concerning lifestyle, many do surprisingly well. As a *group*, however, their work status and employer ratings tend to be somewhat lower than in a comparable group of nonhyperactive adults.

During the course of Bruce's stormy adolescence, his mother consoled herself with the hope that he would outgrow his problems. "I used to say to my husband, 'If we can just hang on until he graduates from high school . . .' He hated school all along. Even when he was just a little kid in second or third grade he never wanted to go. He just couldn't seem to settle down and fit in. Then he started to skip school. He got in with a bad crowd, a group of older fellows who were always in trouble. That's when we started getting calls from the police. Fighting, shoplifting, drinking underage—you name it. You know, the first time we caught him drinking he was only in the seventh grade. His father grounded him for a month.

"But that didn't change anything. He just went on doing anything he pleased, staying out till all hours, coming home drunk or stoned. I know he uses marijuana. I'm sure he uses other drugs, too; I just don't know which ones. I think that's why he can't hold a job. He never lasts longer than a month or a couple of months, at most. He had a good job working construction but they said he was too unreliable—showed up when he felt like it, called in sick a lot.

"I worry about what's going to happen to him. How's he going to support himself? He's twenty-two, and he still acts like he did when he was twelve."

David, a successful engineer, had no trouble describing a hyperactive child: he himself had been one, as was his youngest son, eleven-year-old Scott. At thirty-eight, David still had so much energy that he held a part-time job in addition to his demanding full-time job with a large engineering firm.

Although his own tumultuous childhood and adolescence were far behind him, he still harbored feelings of bitterness and resentment toward his parents, who had tried to control him through harsh physical punishment and ridicule. "They treated me like I was some kind of crazed animal," he recalled. "That's why I don't hit my kids. I don't want them to hate me the way I hated my father."

Despite David's good intentions, however, his family life was frequently unhappy. Although he earned a good income, his impulsive spending habits had brought the family to the brink of financial disaster on several occasions. His hair-trigger temper often frightened the children and reduced his wife to tears. "He's not physical; he never hits me or the boys," his wife explained. "But it's really scary when he blows up. And he's so moody! I never know what to expect when he walks in the door. Sometimes he's down in the dumps for days or even weeks—he won't talk to us; he just goes up to the bedroom and watches television."

"You know," she added, "I really love him. I want this marriage to work: we've been together for sixteen years. But there are times—a lot of times—when I'm very tempted to just pack up the kids and leave him. I know I'd miss him, but the peace and quiet would be great."

PREDICTING ADULT ADJUSTMENT

Predicting which hyperactive youngsters will continue to have trouble as adults is complicated and uncertain because there is not a simple one-to-one relationship between severity of childhood symptoms and overall adult adjustment. Instead, adult adjustment seems to depend on the complex

FACTOR	ADULT ADJUSTMENT	
	GOOD	POOR
Intelligence	Average or above-average intelligence	Below-average intelligence; mentally retarded
Personality traits	Tries to please, concerned with doing well; sensitive to feelings of others; affectionate; feels guilt or remorse for misdeeds	Does not seem to care about approval from others; insensitive or cruel to others; no remorse or guilt
Antisocial behavior	Does not habitually violate major rules (e.g., skip school, steal, run away, use drugs, destroy property); not violent toward others	Habitually violates major rules; defies authority; violent toward others
Family history	No history of alcoholism, mental illness, or antisocial behavior in family members	Mental illness, alcoholism, or antisocial behavior in parents or other family members
Family income, education	Parents well educated, stress importance of education; income sufficient to meet needs of family	Parents poorly educated, do not value education; income below poverty level
Parenting	Firm, consistent discipline coupled with respect for child as a person	Harsh physical punishment; physical or psychological abuse or excessively lax discipline (child allowed to "run wild")

Figure 1. Factors associated with good and poor adult adjustment.

interaction of many factors over the course of time. The most important of these factors are outlined in Figure 1.

Several factors related to the hyperactive child's family and family life form an important cluster that researchers have called the "family support factor." This cluster includes family income and education, mental health of family members, child-rearing practices, and the parent-child relationship. All of these factors influence overall adult adjustment, as well as specific areas of adult functioning. Family income and educational level, for example, are related to educational and work success, with children from affluent, well-educated families faring better than children from the bottom rungs of the socioeconomic ladder. Family income and educational level are also related to antisocial behavior and police involvement. Here again, children from upper socioeconomic levels have a distinct advantage. One reason for this may be that wealthier, better-educated parents have more resources to expend on help for the child.

The most important factor associated with adult antisocial behavior is aggressive, antisocial behavior during childhood. It is a truism that the best way to predict future behavior is to look at past behavior, so we can expect that the child who steals, runs away, is cruel to other children and pets, and generally defies all authority will continue in these patterns when he grows up. These patterns of behavior are found mainly in hyperactive children from families in which other members also engage in antisocial kinds of activities. Quality of parenting is also a factor in adult antisocial behavior; very lax or excessively harsh child-rearing practices, a poor mother-child relationship, and poor mental health of one or both parents increase the likelihood of problems in adulthood.

Personality traits and intelligence are also important predictors of adult adjustment. The combination of aggression, poor tolerance to frustration, and emotional instability does not bode well for the adult years. Hyperactive children with these characteristics are those who are most apt, as adults, to become involved with the police and to show poor emotional adjustment and psychiatric problems. Intelligence is influential in almost every area of adult adjustment and is particularly important in educational achievement.

Frankie was the second of five children born to a high school dropout. His mother, who had her first child when she was sixteen and unmarried, later married Frankie's father and had two children. This marriage ended in divorce when Frankie's father was sentenced to prison for assault. A series of live-in "uncles" followed, and Frankie's mother had two more children, each by a different father. On welfare and struggling with a drug problem, the overwhelmed mother paid little attention to Frankie, who was often left with relatives for weeks at a time.

Frankie's academic career was undistinguished, at best. In elementary school he was frequently sent to the principal's office for disrupting the class, fighting, and violating numerous other school rules. Considered a slow learner, he failed the fourth and sixth grades. By junior high school, he was absent from school more than he was present, and in the tenth grade he simply dropped out of school.

Frankie tried his hand at a series of semiskilled jobs but quit or was fired from all of them after only a few weeks. On one occasion, he was fired on his first day on the job for telling his supervisor, "I don't have to take this shit."

After a long series of skirmishes with the law, dating back to stealing a car at the age of thirteen, Frankie was arrested at nineteen for armed robbery. He was paroled after two years, but within three months he was again arrested. He was convicted of assault with a deadly weapon, among other charges, and was sentenced to ten years in prison.

In recalling his childhood, Ben said, "I know I had some problems but, overall, I'd say my childhood was pretty good." He was the eldest of three children in a close-knit family. His father, an anesthesiologist, was a firm disciplinarian, but he also made it clear that he enjoyed his son's "high spirits" and was proud of his athletic ability.

Active and impulsive from his toddler years, Ben often engaged in daredevil behavior. As a result of his escapades, he had more than his fair share of lumps, bumps, and broken bones. As a preschooler, he painted the dog, the kitchen floor, and most of himself with a can of spray paint. In first grade, he set off a fire alarm, explaining "I wanted to see the fire trucks." The following year, he managed to put his mother's car in gear and smash it into the garage door.

In elementary school, Ben was quickly identified as a bright child. Although his boisterous, impulsive behavior led to many clashes with teachers, his engaging personality inclined most toward tolerance. They were less patient, however, with his incomplete assignments, messy papers, and lost homework. His erratic performance was also a source of frustration to his parents and he was often grounded for poor grades.

Junior high school, when he experimented with truancy and staying out past curfew, was a difficult time for Ben and his family. Then, in high school, his admiration for his biology teacher led him to biology as a career goal. He also needed to keep his grades up in order to play sports, and this, along with his interest in biology, led to improved performance in his last two years of high school.

Although Ben's college career was not an unqualified success, he graduated and found a job in his area of interest. He found the work fascinating and devoted much of his considerable energy to it. His supervisors were impressed by his enthusiasm and high energy, and he received several promotions. After three years, however, he realized that a graduate degree was essential for real advancement in his field, and, with a loan from his parents, he entered graduate school to study for his doctorate.

2

Is My Child Hyperactive?

Diagnosing and Evaluating the Hyperactive Child

HOW DOES A DOCTOR MAKE THE DIAGNOSIS?

To many people, the way in which a psychologist or psychiatrist arrives at a diagnosis is baffling because it seems so different from what they are used to when they go the family doctor with a physical complaint. When you take your child to the pediatrician with an earache or an upset stomach, you know that the doctor will begin by asking about the specific problem: Where does it hurt? When did the pain begin? Has your child had a fever? A change in appetite?

Having taken a history of the problem, the physician proceeds to examine the child, often with the aid of instruments such as a stethoscope and an audioscope. On the basis of this history and his own observations, he narrows down the possible diagnoses. To help confirm his diagnosis, he may order laboratory tests such as blood tests, X rays, and so on. In fact, in our technological society, many people may even be suspicious of the doctor's diagnosis if he does not order such tests.

When a mental health professional is asked to diagnose a behavioral disorder, the methods used are quite different. However, the steps in the diagnostic process—history taking, observation, and testing—are the same.

OBSERVATION

Since there are no physical symptoms like a rash or swollen glands to observe in the case of ADHD, diagnosis can be a confusing matter. ADHD is a far cry from a physical disorder like measles: if a child has measles, he has a fever and red spots whether he is in school, at home, or in the pediatrician's office. In contrast, the child who "has" ADHD may have different symptoms in different settings. Some hyperactive children, called "pervasively hyperactive," do display fairly consistent patterns of overactive, impulsive behavior in virtually all settings. (This is especially common with younger children, particularly if their activity level is very high.)

More commonly, however, hyperactive children are only "situationally hyperactive"; that is, their behavior may vary considerably, depending on the situation. Hyperactive children are usually not so different from other children in active, free-play situations but stick out like "sore thumbs" in structured settings which place constraints on their behavior. For example, a child who is quite active but generally pleasant and agreeable might be considered no problem at home but quite a problem indeed in the classroom, where he is expected to sit quietly in his seat for long periods of time. Similarly, a hyperactive child who is disorganized, absent-minded, and accident-prone can appear quite normal in the pediatrician's office. In fact, a study conducted at the University of Illinois showed that about 80 percent of a large group of hyperactive children did *not* display obvious signs of hyperactivity in the doctor's office. For this reason, doctors cannot limit their diagnosis of ADHD only to those children who appear obviously hyperactive during a single appointment.

This explains why your pediatrician may disagree when you or your child's teachers suspect that your child is hyperactive. It also underscores the need to observe your child in different settings and on different occasions. Practically speaking, your doctor will usually need to consult with you, your child's teachers, baby-sitters, and others who can report on your child's typical behavior in "real-life" settings.

Teachers, in particular, are usually a valuable source of information because it is in school that the hyperactive youngster is apt to have his greatest difficulties. Occasionally a parent is reluctant to allow the mental health professional to contact the child's teacher, fearing that the child will be labeled deviant or mentally disturbed. In most cases, however, teachers are well aware that problems exist, relieved to learn that the parents are seeking help, and more than willing to cooperate with the professional in helping the child.

Some physicians and psychologists prefer to meet in person with the child's teachers and other significant adults in the child's life. If this is not possible, telephone conversations are an acceptable substitute. It is also helpful to have your child's teacher write two or three paragraphs describing your child's strengths and weaknesses as they appear in the school setting. Rating scales, discussed in a later section, are especially useful as a means of obtaining valuable information about the child's behavior in different settings.

TAKING A HISTORY: THE INTERVIEW

In order to formulate a diagnosis, the doctor needs to gather a great deal of information about your child's mental and physical development. To speed up the process, your doctor may ask you to complete questionnaires before the first appointment. It is important that this information be as accurate and as complete as possible. Family albums, if available, can be a useful source of information about developmental milestones and other early life events. You should obtain a complete file of your child's school records, including all report cards, as well as medical records and reports from other mental health professionals who have seen the child in the past.

In addition to questions about your child, the doctor will probably ask many questions about other members of the family. Some of these questions will be rather personal; some —such as questions about depression and alcoholism in the extended family—may seem completely irrelevant to your child's problems. Your doctor is not simply being snoopy, nor is he or she there to judge you in any moral sense.

To help you begin to organize information about your child and your family, a typical questionnaire is provided in Figure 2.

You may wonder whether your child should accompany you to the initial appointment, and you may feel concerned about reciting a laundry list of complaints about your child in his presence. Out of consideration for your child's feelings, your doctor may meet with you alone for the first appointment. This also allows you to talk openly about any personal or family problem that you might be reluctant to discuss in front of your child.

THE PHYSICAL EXAMINATION

With children in whom ADHD is suspected, the physical examination is usually completely normal. It is, however, necessary to rule out a physical disorder as the source of the problem. Lead poisoning, for example, can produce brain damage and symptoms of hyperactivity. Hyperthyroidism is another medical condition characterized by extreme restlessness and emotional ups and downs. Some have suggested that hypoglycemia (low blood sugar) can cause symptoms similar to those of ADHD, and one author described a five-year-old girl whose tantrums, hyperactivity, and school difficulties disappeared following surgery to correct a problem involving

Figure 2. Developmental and Social History Questionnaire.

1. Pregnancy and Delivery
Were there problems during your pregnancy with this child? _____
_____
Problems during delivery? _____
Birthweight _____

2. Infancy
Any illness during newborn period? _____
Was there: _____ Colic _____ Feeding problems
_____ Diarrhea _____ Excessive vomiting
_____ Excessive crying
Other problems or illness during first year? _____
_____
In general, was child: an "easy" baby? _____ a "difficult"
baby? _____

3. Developmental Milestones
Age child: _____ walked alone
_____ spoke in simple sentences
_____ was toilet trained (bowel)
_____ was toilet trained (bladder)
Does child wet _____ or soil _____? During day _____ or night
_____? How often? _____

4. Medical History
Any illness other than normal childhood diseases? _____
Operations/hospitalizations _____
_____
_____ Allergies   _____ Convulsions/seizures
_____ Head Injuries   _____ Frequent colds
_____ Chronic ear infections _____ Eye problems
Is child currently on medication? _____

5. School History
Learning

	Good	Average	Poor
Preschool	_____ Good	_____ Average	_____ Poor
Kindergarten	_____ Good	_____ Average	_____ Poor
Grades 1–3	_____ Good	_____ Average	_____ Poor
Current grade	_____ Good	_____ Average	_____ Poor

Behavior

Preschool	_____ Good	_____ Average	_____ Poor
Kindergarten	_____ Good	_____ Average	_____ Poor
Grades 1–3	_____ Good	_____ Average	_____ Poor
Current grade	_____ Good	_____ Average	_____ Poor

Has child repeated any grades? _____
Is child working at grade level? _____
Have teachers described any of the following classroom problems?

_____ Restless, overactive, out of seat
_____ Inattentive, daydreams, off-task
_____ Doesn't finish work
_____ Impulsive, can't wait his turn
_____ Doesn't do homework

_____ Easily upset, "flies off the handle"
_____ Work sloppy, careless
_____ Needs much attention from teacher
_____ Bothers other children
_____ Uncooperative with teacher

Describe any other school-related problems _____

6. Habits

_____ Temper tantrum
_____ Low frustration tolerance
_____ Accident-prone
_____ Excessively active
_____ Short attention span
_____ Poor memory
_____ Unusual fears

_____ Interrupts frequently
_____ Frequently disobeys
_____ Clumsy
_____ Heedless of danger or consequences
_____ Stealing
_____ Fighting
_____ Poor self-esteem

7. Family and Friends

Describe how child gets along with:
(a) Mother _____
(b) Father _____
(c) Siblings _____
Does child have friends? _____
Child's friends are primarily older _____ younger _____
same age as child _____

8. Major Areas of Concern

What is child's problem? _____

_____

_____

Has child been treated for this problem before? Describe. _____

_____

Has child had psychological testing in school or through a
clinic? _____

_____

9. Family History

Describe any psychiatric problems, drug abuse, or alcoholism in
immediate family and extended family (include grandparents,
cousins, etc.) _____

_____

_____

Has either parent or any of child's blood relatives had a problem
similar to child's? _____
How would you describe your marriage? _____

_____

Do both parents agree concerning child's problem, discipline?

_____

_____

blood flow to the brain. Such cases, however, are probably
very rare.

Recent evidence suggests that sleep apnea can play a role in
some hyperactive patterns of behavior. Sleep apnea is a condition in which the upper airway is blocked during sleep.
Although the obstruction can be due to a variety of causes,
such as oral or facial abnormalities or deposits of too much
soft fatty tissue in the walls of the throat (sometimes seen in
obese children), the most common cause of sleep apnea in
children is enlarged tonsils or adenoids. The obstruction pre-
vents the child from breathing freely during sleep, and the
child often snores loudly and thrashes about as he struggles
to breathe. As a result, of course, he sleeps poorly. Adults
with this disorder often suffer overwhelming sleepiness dur-

ing the day, but in children lack of sleep is more apt to appear as behavioral problems. According to Dr. Richard Ferber, Director of the Center for Pediatric Sleep Disorders at Children's Hospital in Boston,[3] lack of sleep associated with sleep apnea can result in hyperactivity, irritability, difficulty concentrating, forgetfulness, school problems, or general "laziness." Bed wetting may also be seen in children with sleep apnea.

If your child snores loudly, appears to have difficulty breathing during sleep, is very restless during sleep, and has frequent sore throats or ear infections, the possibility of sleep apnea must be explored. If your pediatrician is not familiar with this condition, request a referral to an ear, nose, and throat specialist for his opinion.

When assessing a child in whom ADHD is suspected, many pediatricians include neurological screening as part of the physical examination. This is done to rule out the possibility of a disease of the central nervous system. In the very unlikely event that such a problem were detected, the pediatrician would refer the child to a neurologist for further evaluation. There is no reason to have an electroencephalogram (EEG) done unless your doctor suspects epilepsy.

Although "hard" signs of neurological disease or disorder are not likely to be observed in the hyperactive child, the neurological screening might reveal "soft" signs. This term refers to minor abnormalities in motor, sensory, and integrative function such as poor fine motor coordination, clumsiness, poor balance, impaired hand-eye coordination, and irregular, jerky movements. Doctors think that the presence of soft signs reflects a primary disturbance in the organization of the central nervous system. The disturbance itself might stem from a variety of causes, including mild brain damage or genetic factors. Soft signs may be observed in many otherwise normal children, but they are known to occur with greater than normal frequency in groups of children with learning and behavior problems. Although it has been reported that as many as 50 percent of hyperactive children have neurological soft signs, soft signs have also been noted in children with other kinds of psychiatric disorders. In fact, the latest research suggests that soft signs are associated with an increased vulnerability to psychiatric and learning disorders in general, rather than being associated with any single syndrome. Therefore, the presence of soft signs has very little value in making a specific diagnosis.

Your pediatrician may also check your child for minor physical abnormalities of the head, ears, face, mouth, hands, and feet. Although the incidence of minor abnormalities such as low-set ears, widely spaced eyes, and gaps between the first and second toes is higher than average among hyperactive children, there is also a greater incidence of these abnormalities among other groups of psychiatrically disturbed children. Like neurological soft signs, minor physical anomalies are a kind of nonspecific red flag: their presence indicates that the child is *at risk* for learning problems and psychiatric disorders, but they neither guarantee that the child will develop such problems, nor do they indicate the specific nature of the problems that might occur.

RATING SCALES

Rating scales not only provide a great deal of information in condensed form, they also permit a more precise comparison of your child's behavior with that of his peers. By examining your child's scores on a standardized rating scale, your doctor can say, for example, "In terms of attention span, he has a lower rating than those obtained by 95 percent of children his age."

The best-known and most widely used rating scale for assessing hyperactivity in the school setting is the Conners Teacher Rating Scale. Although researchers often prefer the longer (twenty-eight-item) version, the abbreviated (ten-item) version is more often used in clinical practice, probably because it takes less time. This scale (see Figure 3) is easily scored: each "Very much" is worth three points; each "Pretty

OBSERVATION	DEGREE OF ACTIVITY			
	NOT AT ALL	JUST A LITTLE	PRETTY MUCH	VERY MUCH
1. Restless or overactive				
2. Excitable, impulsive				
3. Disturbs other children				
4. Fails to finish things he starts, short attention span				
5. Constantly fidgeting				
6. Inattentive, easily distracted				
7. Demands must be met immediately, easily frustrated				
8. Cries often and easily				
9. Mood changes quickly and drastically				
10. Temper outbursts; explosive and unpredictable behavior				

Figure 3. Conners Parent/Teacher Rating Scale
(Reprinted with the permission of C. Keith Conners, Ph.D.)

much" is worth two points; and each "Just a little" is worth one point. These scores are then added to obtain a total score.

How should scores on this rating scale be interpreted? In general, scores above 18–20 should make you suspect a diagnosis of ADHD. However, if your child's principal difficulties are in the areas of attention and concentration, even scores as low as 10 or 12 do not mean that you can eliminate the possibility of ADHD.

A new scale which may be more helpful in analyzing classroom behavior is the ADHD Comprehensive Teacher Rating Scale (ACTeRS), developed by researchers at the University of Illinois Institute for Child Behavior and Development. This scale was standardized by administering it to teachers of over a thousand public school children in kindergarten through fifth grade. Using these scores, it is possible to compare your child's scores directly with scores of his peers and eliminate the problem of using a single cutoff score.

The ACTeRS allows for separate examination of four areas of child behavior: attention, hyperactivity, social skills, and oppositional behavior. The questions concerning attention and hyperactivity are reproduced in Figure 4.

Because the authors of this scale believe that inattention is the primary disability in ADHD, their scale was designed to put emphasis on attention. For diagnostic purposes, the authors believe that a poor score on attention is essential for a child to be diagnosed as having ADHD. For girls, a score of 17 places the child just below the 20th percentile, while a score of 14 falls at the 10th percentile. For boys, a score of 15 places the child below the 20th percentile, and a score lower than 13 places the child below the 10th percentile.

The authors state, "If the score is at the 10th percentile or below, no matter what the other scores are, one can confidently feel the diagnosis of ADHD is legitimate." If the score is between the 10th and 25th percentiles, the child *may* warrant a diagnosis of ADHD, depending on his other difficulties. For example, a child who scores at the 20th percentile on

Figure 4. ADD-H Comprehensive Teacher's Rating Scale (ACTeRS).*

Child's name _____ Date _____

Teacher's name _____

Below are descriptions of children's behavior. Please read each item and compare this child's behavior with that of his/her classmates. Circle the numeral that most closely corresponds with your evaluation.

Behavior item	ALMOST NEVER				ALMOST ALWAYS
1. Works well independently	1	2	3	4	5
2. Persists with task for reasonable amount of time	1	2	3	4	5
3. Completes assigned task satisfactorily with little additional assistance	1	2	3	4	5
4. Follows simple directions accurately	1	2	3	4	5
5. Follows a sequence of instructions	1	2	3	4	5
6. Functions well in the classroom	1	2	3	4	5

Add all numbers circled above and place total here...................... Attention _____

	ALMOST NEVER				ALMOST ALWAYS
7. Extremely overactive (out of seat, on the go)	1	2	3	4	5
8. Overreacts	1	2	3	4	5
9. Fidgety (hands always busy)	1	2	3	4	5
10. Impulsive (acts or talks without thinking)	1	2	3	4	5
11. Restless (squirms in seat)	1	2	3	4	5

Add all numbers circled above and place total here.................... Hyperactivity _____

*ACTeRS was developed by Rina K. Ullman, M.Ed., Esther K. Sleator, M.D., and Robert L. Sprague, Ph.D. This portion of it is reprinted with the permission of the publisher and copyright holder, MetriTech, Inc., 111 North Market Street, Champaign, Ill. 61820.

attention but who is also very restless, fidgety, and overactive should probably be diagnosed as having ADHD. If, however, your child's score is higher than the 25th percentile on attention, a diagnosis of ADHD is probably not called for.

Using the ACTeRs scale, it is also possible to compare a child's level of hyperactivity to that of other children. For girs, a score of 15 places the child just below the 20th percentile, while a score of 18 falls at the 10th percentile. For boys, a score of 17 falls below the 20th percentile, while a score of 20 marks the 10th percentile.

Another rating scale used to assess the child's behavior in school is the School Situations Questionnaire, developed by Dr. Russell Barkley. This questionnaire (see Figure 5) lists twelve school situations in which the hyperactive child frequently has problems and asks the teacher to rate the severity of the problem. A score that is as high or higher than scores obtained by 95 percent of school-age children is very strongly suggestive of ADHD. Scores that fall in this range are given below.[4]

Age groups (in years)	Number of problem settings (number of "yes" answers)	Mean severity*
BOYS		
6–8	9	5.5
9–11	9	6.1
GIRLS		
6–8	5	3.8
9–11	5	3.2

* To calculate the mean severity, add all of the numbers circled on the questionnaire and divide the sum by 12.

Rating scales have also been developed to assess ADHD in the home setting, using parents as raters. The most widely used of these scales is the Conners Parent Rating Scale. The

Figure 5. School Situations Questionnaire.

Child's name _____ Date _____

Teacher's name _____

Does this child present any behavior problems for you in any of these situations? if so, indicate how severe they are.

Situation	Yes/No (Circle one)		If "Yes," how severe? (Circle one.) MILD ─────────────── SEVERE
While arriving at school	Yes	No	1 2 3 4 5 6 7 8 9
During individual desk work	Yes	No	1 2 3 4 5 6 7 8 9
During small group activities	Yes	No	1 2 3 4 5 6 7 8 9
During free-play time in class	Yes	No	1 2 3 4 5 6 7 8 9
During lectures to the class	Yes	No	1 2 3 4 5 6 7 8 9
At recess	Yes	No	1 2 3 4 5 6 7 8 9
At lunch	Yes	No	1 2 3 4 5 6 7 8 9
In the hallways	Yes	No	1 2 3 4 5 6 7 8 9
On field trips	Yes	No	1 2 3 4 5 6 7 8 9
During special assemblies	Yes	No	1 2 3 4 5 6 7 8 9
On the bus	Yes	No	1 2 3 4 5 6 7 8 9

(Reprinted with the permission of Russell A. Barkley, Ph.D.)

Figure 6. Home Situations Questionnaire.

Child's name_____   Date _____

Name of person completing this form _____

Does this child present any behavior problems in any of these situations? If so indicate how severe they are.

Situation	Yes/No (Circle one)		If "Yes," how severe? (Circle one.) MILD — SEVERE								
While playing alone	Yes	No	1	2	3	4	5	6	7	8	9
While playing with other children	Yes	No	1	2	3	4	5	6	7	8	9
Mealtimes	Yes	No	1	2	3	4	5	6	7	8	9
Getting dressed	Yes	No	1	2	3	4	5	6	7	8	9
Washing/bathing	Yes	No	1	2	3	4	5	6	7	8	9
While you are on the telephone	Yes	No	1	2	3	4	5	6	7	8	9
While watching TV	Yes	No	1	2	3	4	5	6	7	8	9
When visitors are in your home	Yes	No	1	2	3	4	5	6	7	8	9
When you are visiting someone else	Yes	No	1	2	3	4	5	6	7	8	9
In supermarkets, stores, church, restaurants, or other public places	Yes	No	1	2	3	4	5	6	7	8	9
When asked to do chores at home	Yes	No	1	2	3	4	5	6	7	8	9
At bedtime	Yes	No	1	2	3	4	5	6	7	8	9
While in the car	Yes	No	1	2	3	4	5	6	7	8	9

Situation			MILD								SEVERE
When with a baby-sitter	Yes	No	1 2 3 4 5 6 7 8 9								
When father is home	Yes	No	1 2 3 4 5 6 7 8 9								
When asked to do school homework	Yes	No	1 2 3 4 5 6 7 8 9								

(Reprinted with the permission of Russell A. Barkley, Ph.D.)

ten-item version of this scale is identical in format, content, and scoring to the Teacher Rating Scale (see Figure 2).

Dr. Russell Barkley has also developed a Home Situations Questionnaire (see Figure 6) to be completed by parents.[5] Again, scores which fall at or above the 95th percentile should be considered very strongly suggestive of ADHD. These scores are as follows:

Age groups (in years)	Number of problem settings (number of "yes" answers)	Mean severity*
BOYS		
4–5	8	4.5
6–8	11	4.8
9–11	10	4.9
GIRLS		
4–5	7	4.1
6–8	10	4.6
9–11	9	4.2

* To calculate the mean severity, add all of the numbers circled on the questionnaire and divide the sum by 16.

Rating scales, however useful they may be, are only one of many sources of information used in diagnosing ADHD and should always be used as one of several components of a thorough diagnostic workup. Dr. Conners points out that the most reliable information is obtained when parents and teachers complete the rating scales on two or three occasions about three weeks apart. Although multiple ratings will add to the length of time needed to complete the diagnostic evaluation, the result will be a more accurate picture of the child's behavior. This is particularly important if, as is usually the case, the same scales are later used to evaluate the child's response to medication or other treatments.

When both parents and teachers complete rating scales on the same child, ratings will not always be identical. If, as sometimes happens, parent and teacher ratings differ dramatically, it is usually the teacher who rates the child as more extreme in problem behavior. In this case, it is not a question of who is right and who is wrong. Parents and teachers simply see the child under very different circumstances. Since it is the school setting which places the greatest demands on the child, it is not surprising that his difficulties are usually more obvious when he is at school.

DIAGNOSTIC TESTS

Some parents are dismayed to learn that there are no blood tests or other clinical laboratory tests currently available to detect hyperactivity. Other parents, aware of this, have psychological tests in mind when they ask, "Isn't there some kind of test to find out if my child is hyperactive?"

The principle of psychological tests is simple: just as a physical sample of blood or urine is analyzed in the medical laboratory, samples of behavior are analyzed by means of psychological tests. Psychological tests can be broadly divided into two categories, performance tests and personality tests.

Performance Tests. The performance tests you are probably most familiar with are intelligence tests and achievement tests. Neither type is particularly helpful in making a specific diagnosis of ADHD. However, if school performance is a problem or there is reason to suspect a learning disability, your doctor may find these tests helpful. Among the most commonly used tests are the Wechsler Intelligence Scale for Children (WISC-R), the Wide Range Achievement Test (WRAT), and the Peabody Individual Achievement Tests (PIAT).

Some doctors recommend neuropsychological testing if ADHD is suspected. Neuropsychological tests, designed to diagnose and assess brain damage, may be helpful when there are questions about recovery of skills following an injury. But these tests are quite expensive and are not likely to yield information that can be used in diagnosis or treatment planning for a hyperactive child.

Other kinds of performance tests which may be more helpful in assessing the specific problems associated with ADHD are tests of attention, concentration, and impulsiveness. One of the most commonly used tests, the Continuous Performance Test (CPT), requires the child to watch a screen on which letters or numbers are presented continuously, each appearing for only a few seconds or fractions of a second. The child's task is to press a button only when certain letters or numbers appear. Because the child must pay close attention and avoid pushing the button impulsively in response to incorrect signals, the CPT is considered a test of attention span and impulsiveness.

Although the CPT is not readily available, your doctor may be able to administer it if he has access to a personal computer. He or she may also be able to take advantage of a promising development, the Gordon Diagnostic System. This system consists of two gamelike tasks presented on a small computerlike machine. One task is a continuous performance test. The other task, designed to measure impulsiveness, requires the child to wait for several seconds between responses. These tasks have been standardized on over a thousand children so far, so the child's performance can be compared with that of other children his age.

The Matching Familiar Figures Test (MFFT) is another performance test which has been used to study impulsiveness in

ADHD children. In this test, the child is shown a "target" picture along with a set of similar pictures which contains one that is identical to the target. The child's task is to find the exact match for each of the target pictures. In comparison with other children, hyperactive youngsters typically respond more quickly and make more errors before finding a match.

How helpful are performance tests such as the CPT and the MFFT in diagnosing ADHD? Although these tests appear "scientific," don't be fooled into thinking that they are therefore superior to other sources of information about your child's difficulties. These tests are not infallible, and the results should always be interpreted in the context of other information. For example, when all other evidence points to a diagnosis of hyperactivity, this diagnosis should not be ruled out on the basis of adequate performance on tests on attention span and impulsiveness.

Personality Tests. Personality tests include questionnaires and inventories, usually in true-false or multiple choice format, and so-called "projective tests," such as the Rorschach Inkblot Technique. Projective tests have no "right" or "wrong" answers. Instead, the child must use his imagination to see shapes in the inkblots, or, in the case of the Children's Thematic Apperception Test, to make up stories about pictures. The child's responses and stories, it is thought, reveal his own inner needs, fears, and struggles. Whether or not this approach to personality assessment yields useful information has been the subject of heated controversy for many years. Like neuropsychological tests, projective tests are time-consuming and expensive. Don't be surprised if your doctor feels that the information gained is of no value in diagnosis or treatment planning for your child.

On the other hand, questionnaires and personality inventories could provide useful information about your child. The Personality Inventory for Children (PIC), for example, can distinguish quite well between hyperactive children and nonhyperactive children. It can also reveal other problems in social, academic, and emotional adjustment. Some child psychologists and psychiatrists also use the Children's Incomplete Sentences test, a task which requires the child to respond to phrases such as "My father . . ." and "I hate . . ." by completing the sentence. This information, while not helpful in making a specific diagnosis, can help identify areas of concern and difficulty in the child's life.

COPING WITH A DIAGNOSIS OF ADHD

When a credible professional tells you, "Your child has Attention-deficit Hyperactivity Disorder," a flood of emotions can result. One mother of a hyperactive youngster describes her reaction this way:

"How did I feel when the doctor told me my son was hyperactive? I guess my first reaction was, 'Oh, no, that can't be true!' I had always heard that hyperactive kids were completely out of control, totally wild. There's a little boy in Cal's class who is hyperactive, and he's a monster! Cal certainly isn't like that; in fact, there are lots of times when he's a joy to be with.

"I remember a scared, sinking kind of feeling, too. I think I still wanted to believe that Cal could behave if he really wanted to, if he just tried hard enough. Maybe that was less frightening than the idea of something that neither one of us could really control.

"Jim took it even harder than I did. At first, he just wouldn't accept it. He was angry with the doctor, as if it were somehow the doctor's fault. All along, Jim had said that Cal was just spoiled and that if we—meaning me—cracked down on him, he'd shape up. Now here was this doctor telling us that it wasn't me, it wasn't us, it wasn't Cal's teachers: something really was wrong with our little boy.

"I think that one of the reasons that it hit Jim so hard was because his parents were told that he was a hyperactive kid. He had a lot of problems growing up, and I know he's afraid that Cal will have to go through the same things. I think he feels guilty, too, like it's his fault for passing this on to his son."

Many parents of hyperactive children experience at least some of the feelings described by this mother. Children, too, may react with strong feelings, although these feelings seldom surface in the doctor's office. In fact, in front of the doctor, many hyperactive children will steadfastly deny that they have any problems, at least until they are very comfortable with the doctor. As Dr. Paul Wender[6] points out, this denial is an attempt to save face, and I agree with Dr. Wender that it is not really necessary that the child admit his difficulties to the doctor.

Children who are reluctant to air their problems in front of a professional can usually talk much more openly with their parents. Don't be surprised, however, if your child is not ready to discuss his feelings right away, even with you. If he seems indifferent or uninterested, he may simply need a bit of time to mull things over before he is ready to talk about his questions and concerns. You can leave the door to communication open by suggesting that, if questions do occur to him, you would like to hear them.

Compared with younger children, teenagers are often more willing to acknowledge their difficulties. Many teenagers, in fact, are relieved when a name is finally given to their problem and are eager to find out as much as possible about the disorder. With teenagers, it is often helpful to refer to differences in brain biochemistry to explain the disorder (see Chapter 3). As Dr. Wender points out, this exempts the young person from "moral blameworthiness."

I agree wholeheartedly with Dr. Wender, but in my practice I do not limit the use of this explanation to teenagers. I have found that even young children can understand the analogy of a car that is out of gas. The brain, I explain, is a complicated and wonderful machine but, just like a car, it needs fuel to operate properly.

"What happens when a car runs out of gas?" I ask.

"It won't go," is the inevitable response.

"Right, it won't go. Does that mean that there is something wrong with the car—that it's a bad car?"

"No."

"No, there's nothing wrong with the car. It can be a great car, a super car. But it won't work without the right kind of fuel, will it?"

I go on to explain that the child's brain is just like that car: it may be a super brain, but it isn't getting the kind of fuel it needs to make it work as well as it should. With older children and teenagers, I provide more technical details and supplement my explanation with pictures and diagrams of neurons, neuronal transmission, and so on.

Because children dread being different from their friends, it is sometimes helpful to tell the child that he is certainly not the only one with his particular problems. While younger children can't appreciate numerical concepts expressed as percentages, many can grasp the picture if they are told that one child in thirty—or one in every classroom in his school— has similar problems.

I also tell children about eminent people who have had ADHD. Thomas Edison, for example, was constantly in trouble as a child and was removed from school after attending for only three months. Former governor and U.S. Senator Huey Long was also a hyperactive child, as was Winston Churchill. While this information is not comforting to every child (one of my young patients objected, "Yeah, but they're famous— and I'm not!"), some hyperactive youngsters do enjoy reading biographies of famous people who had problems similar to their own. Reading about people who have overcome these difficulties can help both you and your child maintain greater optimism and a more positive attitude toward overcoming problems.

3

What Causes Hyperactivity?

If your child has been diagnosed as hyperactive, you naturally wonder what went wrong, and you've probably come up with your own theories to explain the causes of his unruly behavior. You may suspect environmental causes. "Maybe he has food allergies," many parents suggest, or, "The school demands too much (or not enough) of him." Some parents blame traumatic events in the child's life. "He was fine until we moved here from New Jersey," they say, or "He's never gotten over his grandfather's death three years ago."

Most commonly, parents assume that they themselves are at fault; that something they have done or failed to do lies at the heart of the problem. "We spoiled him" is a common explanation. Parents are especially apt to assume blame or to blame each other if there has been a divorce or if one parent suffers from alcoholism, depression, or another psychiatric disorder.

ARE PARENTS TO BLAME?

Among today's parents, the prevailing view seems to be that infants are like formless lumps of clay that are shaped and molded by life experiences, especially those which occur in the early years. According to this theory, if parents are "good" parents—if they use the right child-rearing methods and have a sound relationship with their child—the child will grow up to be happy, successful, and well adjusted. On the other hand, if the child turns out poorly—if he drops out of school, can't hold a job, takes drugs, and so on—then parents are to blame. This notion, which has its roots in the theories of Sigmund Freud, is widespread in Western cultures.

The theory that parental behavior determines child adjustment has received very strong support from professionals in child mental health. Many mental health professionals (particularly those trained in the Freudian approach) minimize the importance of biological factors and emphasize the importance of early life experiences in determining personality and psychological adjustment. In fact, some have even suggested that poor parenting actually *causes* such disorders as ADHD.

Is there evidence to support this suggestion? Clinical psychologist Russell Barkley, widely known and respected for his scholarly research with hyperactive children and their families, thinks not.[7] If poor parenting were to blame, he asks, how can we explain why the child's problems are often apparent from the earliest days of life and extend across so many situations? Nor can this theory explain the high incidence of learning disabilities, minor physical anomalies, and frequent illnesses in infancy among hyperactive children. Finally, Barkley points out, the theory cannot account for the fact that many parents of hyperactive children have been successful in raising other children who appear quite well adjusted and have no symptoms of ADHD.

Concerning the last point, researchers have counterargued

that differences between the way parents relate to their hyperactive children and the way they relate to their other children result in differences in child personality and behavior. It is true, as parents of hyperactive children know from experience, that they do behave differently toward a hyperactive child. Barkley observed parents interacting with their hyperactive and nonhyperactive children and found that when parents interact with their hyperactive child, they are more controlling and negative, issuing more commands and prohibitions. They are also less responsive to the hyperactive child's requests for attention than to the same behavior in their other children. Barkley also looked at patterns of child behavior and found that, compared to the way in which other youngsters interacted with their parents, hyperactive children were considerably more negative and disobedient.

Many mental health professionals have concluded that parents are therefore the cause of the child's difficult behavior. The child's behavior, they reason, is simply a predictable reaction to negative and overcontrolling parental behavior.

The flaw in this logic, however, is the assumption that the influence is in one direction only—from parent to child—and that child behavior has no effect on parent reactions. Children are **not** merely "blank slates" upon which experience writes. Parents have always known what research has only recently revealed: infants are born with individual personal styles, or temperaments, which are obvious from the first weeks of life. Some are placid and easygoing right from the start. When a diaper is wet or a feeding is delayed, they make their needs known with whimpers or quiet cries. Other babies are much more vigorous and intense. If their needs are not met quickly, they burst into red-faced screams. Similarly, while some infants easily settle into a predictable routine of eating, sleeping, and eliminating, others are very irregular in their habits and never seem to develop regular routines.

These and other patterns of temperament were investigated in the New York Longitudinal Study,[8] a fascinating investigation that followed a large group of children from birth through late adolescence. This research revealed that, from birth, children show distinctive temperaments that tend to be fairly stable over many years. The researchers were able to identify three major temperamental styles:

• *Easy children* accounted for about 40 percent of those in the study group. These children are generally positive in mood, adjust well to change, and quickly adapt to schedules and routines. The intensity of their reactions tends to be mild or moderate, and, when such a child does cry, it is usually a signal that something is indeed amiss.

• *Slow-to-warm-up children* dislike change. They typically react to new situations—the first bath, strangers, new foods—by quietly withdrawing. However, if they are allowed to proceed at their own pace, they gradually make a good adjustment to a new situation.

• *Difficult children,* who comprised about 10 percent of the study group, have great difficulty settling into a predictable routine. Their mood is generally negative, and they react poorly to new situations. Their reactions are often forceful and intense, and their activity level is high. These children are particularly prone to develop behavioral disturbances, and a difficult temperament is characteristic of many hyperactive children.

How does the behavior of a difficult infant affect the way his parents interact with him? Parents who have coped with a difficult child can testify that such a child can drive even the most patient of parents to the brink of despair. Many say that they quickly learned to treat their difficult child differently from their other children because his behavior demanded a different approach.

"I've always been a stickler about table manners, but I've just given up with Sandy. So most of her dinner lands in her lap—

who cares? I'm happy if she'll just sit still long enough to get a few bites in her mouth."

"We never have bedtime problems with Cathy or Jack; a story, a goodnight kiss, turn out the lights, and that's it. Mike is a different story. If one of us doesn't lie down with him for an hour or so, he's out of bed every five minutes."

"I know all the other children in the neighborhood are allowed to go to the playground by themselves at his age. But if I'm not right there to watch him, you can bet Brian will get into some kind of trouble within the first ten minutes."

If interaction between parents and their children is a two-way street, it is logical to ask whether the behavior of a hyperactive child's parents is at least partly a response to the child's behavior. Do hyperactive children *teach* their parents to be overly controlling and negative, perhaps after countless repetitions of "Stop that," "Leave that alone," and "Don't do that"?

Dr. Russell Barkley's research forms convincing evidence that the behavior of the hyperactive child directly affects the way his parents treat him. In a half dozen studies, Dr. Barkley has shown that when medication produces changes in child behavior, there is an immediate change in parent behavior. As the child's negative, disobedient behavior changes to more positive and obedient, his parents' behavior changes accordingly. These findings certainly suggest that many parents of hyperactive children learn to be overly controlling as a means of managing their child's difficult behavior. It is encouraging to find, however, that these patterns are not set in cement and that changes in the child can bring about very marked changes in the parent.

While poor child-rearing practices do *not* cause ADHD, this certainly does not mean that child-rearing practices have no effect on the behavior of the hyperactive child. Harsh, punitive tactics—beatings, whippings, name calling—do little to control hyperactive behavior and only worsen the child's poor self-esteem. On the other hand, the parent who simply gives up and lets his hyperactive child "run wild" does the child no favor. Just like any other child, the hyperactive child needs consistent discipline coupled with respect for the child as a person. This means clear limits and appropriate rewards and penalties. Some helpful suggestions are discussed in Chapter 5.

WAS MY CHILD BORN THIS WAY?

Many hyperactive children come into the world with a difficult temperament and other problems. This has led scientists to suggest that something goes amiss during the nine months before birth (prenatal period) or during the birth process itself (perinatal period). The research of Doctors Carolyn Hartsough and Nadine Lambert[9] at Berkeley, begun a decade ago, yields some clues about this issue. The researchers examined the medical histories of 300 hyperactive children. For purposes of comparison, they also examined the medical histories of 190 normal children. When the groups were compared, several differences emerged.

• *Maternal health during pregnancy.* The mothers of hyperactive children were more likely to report poor health during pregnancy.

• *Age of mother.* A higher percentage of mothers of hyperactive children were under the age of twenty when the child was born.

• *First pregnancy.* Hyperactive children were more likely than other children to have been firstborns.

• *Toxemia or eclampsia.* Mothers of hyperactive children more frequently reported toxemia (an infection which results in bacterial toxins circulating in the bloodstream) or eclampsia (coma or convulsions associated with high blood pressure, fluid retention, and/or abnormal proteins in the urine).

• *Long labor.* Mothers of hyperactive children were more likely to have had labor lasting longer than thirteen hours.

• *Fetal distress.* Hyperactive children were twice as likely to have evidence of fetal distress, head injuries, or other birth injuries.

• *Postmaturity.* More hyperactive children were born at a gestational age of ten months or later. (Interestingly, the groups did not differ in the frequency of prematurity or low birthweight.)

• *Congenital problems.* Hyperactive children more frequently had medical problems or physical malformations at birth.

Doctors Hartsough and Lambert are not alone in finding a relationship between ADHD and the prenatal and perinatal problems they have identified: other scientists have reported similar findings. Some have also drawn a connection between ADHD and maternal alcohol abuse during pregnancy. Others have implicated heavy maternal smoking during pregnancy.

It is very important to stress, however, that not all hyperactive children—not even the majority—have histories of prenatal or perinatal problems, and not all children with prenatal or perinatal problems become hyperactive. Problems during or before birth are not the sole cause of ADHD. However, it appears that for a small number of hyperactive children, early damage may have rendered them vulnerable to a variety of disorders, including ADHD.

IS IT SOMETHING IN HIS ENVIRONMENT?

Damage to the child's developing nervous system can occur after birth as well as before birth. The potential sources of such damage include a great number of hazardous substances in our environment. Asbestos, foam insulation, toxic wastes dumped into rivers and leaking from underground storage tanks, high levels of pollutants in the air—all are now known to pose serious hazards to our health.

The effects of lead poisoning have long been known, and lead poisoning has been suggested by many as a possible cause of ADHD. In addition to fatigue, pallor, irritability, nausea, and loss of appetite, lead poisoning can result in neurological damage and psychological problems. In fact, among children with confirmed lead poisoning, about one third have symptoms of ADHD.

A great deal of research has been done on the relationship between high lead levels in the body and hyperactivity. Unfortunately, the questions of how to measure lead levels in the body and "how much is too much" have not really been answered, so it is too early to draw firm conclusions. For most hyperactive children, however, it is unlikely that lead is the source of the problem.

As Americans have become more knowledgeable about the environmental hazards around them, many have become concerned about the possible dangers of food additives. Over four thousand chemicals are used in food processing, including artificial flavors, dyes to enhance appearance, and preservatives to extend shelf life. Food dyes are even used to enhance the appearance of dog food, despite the fact that dogs are color-blind!

Dr. Benjamin Feingold, a pediatrician and allergist, was the first to draw widespread attention to the idea that food dyes and additives might cause ADHD and other behavior disorders. In fact, Dr. Feingold speculated that allergylike reactions to certain foods and food additives cause about half of the cases of ADHD in this country. In addition to synthetic dyes and flavorings, Dr. Feingold believed that intolerance to salicylates, an acidic substance found in aspirin and many fruits and vegetables, could also result in behavioral disturbances.

Dr. Lendon Smith had a similar theory. He argued that consumption of junk food and large quantities of refined sugar can cause ADHD, as well as all sorts of other behavioral and emotional problems in children. Dr. Smith's theories became well known through his books, *Improving Your Child's Behavior Chemistry* and *Feed Your Kids Right*.

The theories of Feingold and Smith are appealing, especially to a public grown wary of pollutants, chemicals, drugs, and food additives. However, as noted authority Dr. John Werry points out, "The scientific status [of these theories] is piffle!" Although hyperactive children do have more allergies, including food allergies, than other children, only a few improve significantly on additive-free diets. And, in spite of the enormous popularity of Dr. Smith's theories, studies have now shown that refined sugar has nothing to do with symptoms of hyperactivity in children. (Both subjects are discussed in greater detail in Chapter 4.) Thus, it appears highly unlikely that food allergies, nutritional deficiencies, or reactions to sugar are responsible for your child's hyperactivity.

IS IT HEREDITARY?

A surprising number of parents of hyperactive children describe their child as "a chip off the old block," adding, "He's the spitting image of me when I was a child." Some parents are not amused by the family resemblance: "He's nothing but trouble, just like his no-good father," or "What can you expect with a mother like that!"

Does ADHD "run in families," like diabetes and other disorders which have a genetic component? In some families, this certainly seems to be the case. Compared with parents of other children, parents of hyperactive children are much more likely—as much as ten times more likely, in fact—to have been hyperactive children themselves. If the child is severely hyperactive, the likelihood that one or both parents was hyperactive may be even greater, according to Dr. Leopold Bellack at New York University. Among the hyperactive children he has examined, Dr. Bellack states, "In severe cases of ADHD, I found heavy involvement every time in both parents and the parents' families."[10]

Siblings (especially brothers) of hyperactive children are also more likely than other children to have symptoms of ADHD: as many as one fourth of the brothers of hyperactive children have similar problems themselves. The risk appears greatest for children who have a hyperactive twin. Researchers have studied a small group of hyperactive children with identical twins. In every case, the twin was also hyperactive.

Other problems also seem to run in the families of hyperactive children. For example, doctors often discover alcoholism in parents, grandparents, and other relatives. They sometimes also find antisocial behavior in the family, but this is almost always in the case of hyperactive children who themselves engage in antisocial behavior. Depression also occurs more frequently in families of hyperactive children than in the general population. All of these disorders are the same as those to which hyperactive children themselves are prone as adolescents and adults.

Since many hyperactive children grow up in families in which one or more members has a psychiatric illness, does this mean that there is a hereditary component in ADHD? Or are the hyperactive child's difficulties due instead to the stress of growing up in a disturbed family? Perhaps the child has simply learned troublesome behavior patterns from a parental role model, just as other children learn by imitating their parents. A look at studies of adopted hyperactive children, raised from infancy by people who were not their biological parents, can help answer these questions.

Researchers estimate that as many as 20 percent or more of adopted children are hyperactive, compared with only 3 to 5 percent of children in general. I have seen many adopted children in my practice and, like others who work with hyperactive children, I have long been aware of the frequency with which we see ADHD in this group. (I have also been quite dismayed at how many of these children were previously diagnosed only as suffering from emotional problems supposedly stemming from the fact that they were adopted, with no recognition of the ADHD itself.)

We can't really explain the high incidence of ADHD among adopted children, but we do know that many children who are put up for adoption are born to very young mothers—a risk factor for ADHD—or to parents who are in some other way too incapacitated to care for a child. In fact, we know that there is a *higher than average* incidence of ADHD and related disorders among the biological parents and other blood relatives of adopted hyperactive children. In the adoptive families, on the other hand, the incidence of these disorders in generally quite *low*. This is especially true among the adoptive parents themselves because most people with psychiatric disorders, alcoholism, and antisocial behavior are screened out during the adoption process. From this, it appears that heredity has a stronger influence on ADHD than does environment.

Although not all cases of ADHD involve heredity, the evidence points to the role of genetic factors in many cases. But what is it that the hyperactive child inherits? New research on the brain and behavior, discussed in the following section, suggests some answers to this question.

IS IT CAUSED BY DISTURBANCES IN THE BRAIN?

As the older terms "minimal brain damage" and "minimal brain dysfunction" suggest, scientists have long suspected that the hyperactive child's difficulties might stem from brain malfunction. Hundreds of research studies have addressed this question, but advances in our actual knowledge have come very slowly. Progress has been hindered by the incredible complexity and delicacy of the brain itself. To understand the difficulties faced by those who study the brain, it is useful to know a bit about the brain and how it works.

THE BRAIN: PIECES OF THE PUZZLE

The brain consists of billions of nerve cells, each of which has hundreds of connections with other nerve cells. (So complex is the human brain, in fact, that the number of possible interconnections among the cells in a single human brain is greater than the number of atomic particles that constitute the entire universe!) Groups of cells form highly specialized control centers within the brain. Fibers extending from nerve cells in these centers from pathways throughout the brain, linking the control centers to each other.

Each nerve cell consists of a cell body and a long projection, called the "axon," that is used to communicate with other nerve cells. When a nerve cell fires, the message is sent along the axon through a process of electrical conduction. When the electrical impulse reaches the end of the axon, it causes storage sacs in the end of the axon to release a substance called a "neurotransmitter." This substance crosses the tiny space that separates the axon from the body of the next cell. There it excites a receptor on the cell body and causes that cell to fire, in turn.

After the message has been chemically transmitted, the neurotransmitter must somehow be removed from the locale of the receptor, or it would continue to send the message forever. One method of removal is called "reuptake": the neurotransmitter travels back to the sending cell and is taken up into the storage sacs again. Another means by which neurotransmitters are removed is through chemical breakdown and deactivation.

Neuroscientists now believe that mental disorders are caused by breakdowns or imbalances in neurotransmitter systems. From this point of view, the treatment of mental disorders involves correcting these chemical imbalances through the use of drugs. Drugs that have an influence on the brain can exert their effects in a variety of ways. Some drugs interfere with the production of certain neurotransmitters, resulting in lower levels of these messenger chemicals in the brain. Other drugs increase the production of specific neurotransmitters or mimic the action of natural neurotransmitters; this has the same effect of increasing the amount of the substance available in the brain. Drugs can also exert an effect by preventing reuptake of the neurotransmitter back into storage sacs or by interfering with the breakdown of neurotransmitters. In both cases, the result is a net increase in the amount of active neurotransmitter at the receptor site. Still other drugs work by influencing the sensitivity of particular receptors, making them more or less responsive to incoming messages.

THE BRAIN AND BEHAVIOR IN ADHD

Although the basic structure of the brain in the hyperactive child appears to be intact—there are no obvious malformations or missing parts—this does not eliminate more subtle deviations in brain function. These subtle differences, while difficult to detect with our current techniques, may account for dramatic differences in behavior and emotion. Within the past few years, increasing technological sophistication has enabled us to make great strides in our knowledge about the brain and behavior.

Some of the earlier scientific attempts to explore the question of brain abnormalities in hyperactive children used electroencephalography (EEG) to measure electrical activity in the brain. Electroencephalography involves placing electrodes on the skull to record the electrical activity which occurs when messages are communicated from brain cell to brain cell. Because the EEG measures electrical activity only on the surface of the brain and because it summarizes the electrical activity of millions of nerve cells, it is a relatively crude technique for examining the brain. Therefore, although the EEG is useful in diagnosing certain neurological disorders such as epilepsy (a condition in which large groups of brain cells fire wildly, producing "electrical storms" in the brain), it is not helpful in detecting more subtle abnormalities in brain function.

More recently, researchers have turned their attention to altered brain biochemistry as a factor in ADHD. The fact that certain kinds of stimulants can produce marked changes in the behavior of the hyperactive child has encouraged scientists to search for underlying abnormalities in neurotransmitter systems. Here again, however, researchers have been frustrated by the limited tools and techniques available. Because they cannot directly assess neurotransmitters in the human brain, scientists must rely on indirect measures, such as levels of neurotransmitter breakdown products in blood, urine, and spinal fluid. Unfortunately, we cannot be absolutely certain what these measures really mean in terms of brain function because we have no way of knowing what parts of the brain produced which biochemicals. (In fact, we cannot even be sure how much of a particular biochemical was produced in the brain, because other organs in the body also manufacture and release similar substances.) Therefore, although there have been reports of differences in brain biochemical levels in hyperactive children, it is unlikely that current techniques will yield much useful information.

More promising approaches to the study of brain abnormalities in hyperactive children involve the new techniques of brain imaging. The most familiar of these techniques is the computerized tomography (CT) scan, which uses X rays to construct a computerized image of the brain. Unlike traditional X ray techniques, which do not give a clear picture of brain structure, the CT technique provides a very vivid image of the brain.

Other brain imaging techniques go a step further: instead of allowing us to see only the structure of the brain, techniques such as measuring blood flow in various sections of the brain give us the chance to observe the brain when it is actually at work. To measure blood flow in different regions of the brain, radioactive substances are used as "tracers" in the blood circulating in the brain. CT scan techniques are then used to detect these tracers, and, from this, scientists can determine the amount of blood flowing through different parts of the brain. Because patients are exposed to some radiation, the use of this technique in research with children is sharply restricted in this country. In Denmark, however, a group of scientists who used this technique to study a group of hyperactive children found reduced blood flow in the frontal lobes of the brain in every child they examined. After treatment with Ritalin, a medication commonly used to treat hyperactive children, all of the children showed increased blood flow in the affected areas.[11]

In the United States, although scientists have not been able to use the new methods to study the hyperactive child's brain at work, other avenues are being explored. Brain imaging studies of hyperactive adults are now in progress at the National Institute of Mental Health in Bethesda, Maryland. These studies, under the direction of psychiatrist Alan Zametkin, are based on the ultimate in new brain imaging techniques, the PET scan. The term "PET" stands for "positron emission tomography"; radioactive substances that emit positrons are used to label glucose so it can be traced in the brain. When the glucose is taken up by the brain and used as fuel, the most active parts of the brain use the largest amounts of glucose. Using devices to detect radioactivity, scientists can then determine which parts of the brain are most active when the brain is at work.

Although it is still too early to know the results of the PET-scan studies, the findings from the Danish researchers give us important clues about the cause of ADHD. Certainly, they fit well with what we know about the frontal lobes of the brain. We know, for example, that the frontal lobes are involved in regulating attention, activity, and emotional reactions. When these areas are destroyed in laboratory monkeys, the monkeys become hyperactive, distractible, and emotionally overreactive—much like the hyperactive child. We also know that the frontal lobes are involved in the ability to plan ahead, another area in which hyperactive children typically have problems.

Interestingly, this area of the brain does not seem to be associated with intelligence, at least not with the kind of intelligence our intelligence tests measure. People who have suffered disease or damage to the frontal lobes make perfectly normal scores on most standard intelligence tests. These people do, however, undergo subtle but quite consistent personality changes and are described as emotionally overreactive and lacking in initiative, planning ability, and foresight. They may also be irritable and rather bad-tempered. Also, people with frontal lobe damage seem to be unable to control their impulsive actions. Although they are quite capable of understanding and even describing the rules in a given situation, they appear incapable of abiding by the rules. This impulsiveness is revealed not only in laboratory tests, but also in their behavior in real life. Of course, this inability to follow the rules is also one of the major problems found in hyperactive children.

In my opinion, the evidence strongly suggests that the symptoms of ADHD are caused by malfunction in the frontal areas of the brain. In some hyperactive children, the malfunction might be due to heredity. In others, the malfunction may have been caused by problems before birth or by injury during birth. Still other hyperactive children may have developed problems as a result of head injury, lead poisoning, or exposure to other toxins during their first years of life.

Whether or not you can pinpoint the likely cause of your child's hyperactivity is probably not important. What *is* important for you and your child is that our accumulating knowledge about ADHD and the brain points to a better understanding of ADHD and better methods of treating it.

4

What Can We Do About It?

Medical Treatment of Attention-deficit Hyperactivity Disorder

The physical methods used in the treatment of ADHD have long been controversial. Stimulant medication, in particular, has been the subject of intense—but not always well-informed —debate. Inaccurate news stories have often generated more heat than light as when, in 1970, the Washington *Post* erroneously reported that 5–10 percent of schoolchildren in Omaha, Nebraska, were taking stimulant medication to improve their behavior. (This figure, it was later revealed, represented the estimated number of learning-disabled children in Omaha, *not* the number receiving stimulant medication.) Despite the many careful scientific studies in which stimulant medication has been shown to be helpful, misconceptions still abound.

Diet, too, has received a great deal of attention as a means of treating ADHD. Contending that food additives are a leading cause of hyperactivity, allergist Benjamin Feingold popularized the so-called "Feingold Diet" (sometimes called the Kaiser-Permanente Diet). Although research findings do not support Dr. Feingold's claims, bookstores continue to stock ample supplies of advice-to-parents books touting this and other diets as cures for ADHD.

There *are* treatment methods that can help hyperactive children. Sadly, however, many hyperactive children are denied the opportunity to benefit from these treatments because their parents have been misled by myths and misinformation. Don't let this happen to your child. Don't let misinformation stand in the way of getting the most effective help for your hyperactive child.

STIMULANT MEDICATION

Half a century ago, the startling discovery was made that central nervous system stimulants such as amphetamine had the unexpected effect of calming restless, hyperactive children. Dr. Charles Bradley, a physician who was among the first to report this remarkable observation, gave Benzedrine (amphetamine) to a group of behavior-disordered youngsters and noted, "A large proportion of the children became emotionally subdued without, however, losing interest in their surroundings. . . . Possibly the most spectacular change in behavior . . . was the remarkable improvement in school performance of approximately half of the children."[12]

Bradley's discovery was generally ignored for years. Then, in the 1950s, the development of potent new drugs which offered hope for the mentally ill stimulated renewed interest among doctors working with hyperactive children. Many scientific studies confirmed Bradley's findings, and the stimulants Dexedrine (dextroamphetamine) and Ritalin (methylphenidate) came into common use for the treatment of ADHD.

Today, many consider drug treatment to be the most effective form of treatment for ADHD. Certainly, with an estimated 1–2 percent of elementary school children receiving stimulant medication, it is the most common form of treat-

ment for this condition. Ritalin is the most frequently prescribed, followed by Dexedrine. Cylert (magnesium
pemoline), a relative newcomer, is used somewhat less often
because the effects are not obvious for a period of days or
weeks. However, Cylert can be a very effective alternative for
many children who do not respond to Ritalin or Dexedrine.

How Do Stimulant Drugs Work?

When the doctor tells you that medication might help your
hyperactive child, you might assume that a tranquilizer or a
sedative is intended. You might be astonished at the idea of
giving a stimulant to a child who is already too active and
energetic, and you probably wonder, "How can a stimulant
slow him down?"

The answer is that stimulants do not simply "slow down" or
sedate the hyperactive child. Instead, they help the child focus
his attention and regulate his activity level. They also help
him regulate his behavior so that it is less disorganized and
chaotic. Although stimulants may make adults feel happy or
euphoric, children do not report this effect. Instead, they may
describe feeling "funny" or "tired." (This may explain why,
among all of the thousands of children taking stimulant medication for ADHD, there is only one reported case of a youngster who abused medication for pleasure.)

How do stimulants work to help hyperactive children? The
exact mechanism is not yet known, but all of the evidence
points to an effect on the neurotransmitters, the chemical
messengers in the brain. This means that stimulants do not
merely mask or cover up the symptoms of ADHD, as some
believe. Instead, because they correct a biochemical problem,
they act directly on the disorder itself.

Beneficial Effects

When hyperactive children are treated with stimulant medication, 70–80 percent or more show improvement across a

broad range of behavior. When improvement occurs, it is immediate and sometimes quite dramatic.

One of the most obvious changes you can expect is better regulation of physical activity. It is important to stress that hyperactive children treated with medication are not simply less active across the board, as we would see in sedated children. In an active play situation, when boisterous, exuberant behavior is expected and acceptable, you will see no changes in your child's behavior. However, in settings which call for more restrained behavior, you can expect less fidgeting and hopping about.

When eight-year-old Jimmy was diagnosed as hyperactive and the recommendation was made for a trial of Ritalin, his parents were at first reluctant to put their child "on drugs." After much deliberation, they agreed on a two-week trial of medication, but, as his mother stated skeptically, "We're not so sure that this is a great idea."

Two weeks later, they returned for another appointment, bringing with them a sheaf of notes. "You know," Jimmy's mother began, "we had a lot of reservations about this, but he does seem much calmer on the medicine. We noticed a big difference in his behavior in church: he actually sat through the service for two Sundays in a row without a major scene."

"And that trip to see your aunt last weekend—he wasn't all over the car, giving me fits," Jimmy's father broke in.

Jimmy's teachers had also noticed a change, they added. Jimmy was now able to sit at his desk and finish his work without constant trips to the bathroom, the pencil sharpener, and the teacher's desk. Even the school bus driver commented on the improvement: "He thought Jimmy must be coming down with the flu or something because he didn't have to yell at him for bouncing on the seats or jumping in the aisles."

In addition to better control of activity level, your child should also be in better control of his tendency to behave impulsively. You might observe that he is more likely to resist temptation and that he can conform to rules that were ignored in the past. The child who previously butted into every conversation and shoved his way to the front of every line, for example, can now wait his turn with a semblance of grace. One mother reported with delight, "I can actually carry on a phone conversation or have a friend over for coffee without a thousand interruptions."

Parents of younger children may be particularly relieved at the youngster's newfound ability to keep his hands to himself in stores. Many parents of older children report that the child is less likely to take the belongings of other family members without asking permission. Food hoarding, an unusual but bothersome symptom seen occasionally in hyperactive children, stops in response to stimulant treatment, although repeated attempts to end the behavior through punishment and other measures may have met with failure over a period of many years. Because the child is less impulsive and active, there may be fewer accidents involving bodily harm and damage to property. One parent described these changes by saying, "It's not just what he does that's changed; it's the way he does it. He can walk instead of run or jump or stomp; close doors without slamming them; turn off a lamp without knocking it over."

Your child's teacher will probably be pleased because the child no longer calls out impulsively in class or starts to work before the teacher finishes giving directions. She may also describe a more careful and deliberate approach to tasks so that fewer careless errors mar the child's work. In addition, there may be a marked improvement in your child's handwriting.

In the laboratory, tests show beneficial effects of stimulant drugs on attention span and concentration, while in the classroom, teachers report:

"He works more, daydreams less—much less time frittered away gazing out the window."

"She pays attention to her work rather than chatting with neighbors or bothering the child next to her."

"He works carefully now, with fewer careless mistakes."

Recent research also reveals improved performance in reading, spelling, and arithmetic.* In one study, for example, medication resulted in a 30 percent increase in the number of arithmetic problems completed, with no loss in accuracy.

Overall, parents and teachers describe a child who is less absentminded and disorganized. No longer does the child ask to have instructions repeated a second, third, or even fourth time; because he is better able to focus his attention, he is more likely to absorb the information when it is given the first time. Dawdlers and daydreamers may show improvement in their ability to follow through on routines, such as setting the table or getting dressed (although morning dawdling may remain a problem, depending on the time medication is taken).

In addition to improvements in hyperactivity, inattention, and impulsiveness, stimulant medication also helps such symptoms as aggressive behavior and poor tolerance of frustration. You may notice that your child seems more capable of coping with disappointment; less likely to burst into angry tears when thwarted in his efforts or denied a request. He may handle difficult situations like being teased by siblings with greater poise. "He's learning to walk away or come tell me when his sister bugs him," reported the mother of a hyperactive child who had been known to attack his sister with rocks and, on one occasion, a fireplace poker. Another parent observed, "He doesn't fall apart at little things anymore, and he doesn't go completely out of control if he can't have his own

---

* However, this does not necessarily ensure long-term gains in academic achievement for all ADHD children. For discussion, see the following section, "What Stimulant Medication Cannot Do."

way. Oh, he still gets angry and stomps around, but now it's just normal kid stuff."

With many hyperactive children, one important change may be in the area of social interaction. In his laboratory at the Medical College of Wisconsin, Dr. Russell Barkley studied how Ritalin affects the way hyperactive children and their parents interact and reported immediate reductions in parent-child conflict. In the classroom, too, social relations improve because teachers reduce their controlling, disciplinary actions as the child's behavior improves. Better relations with other children have also been reported. Again, this appears to be a two-way street: as the hyperactive child behaves in a less bossy and demanding fashion, there is a corresponding improvement in the way other children react to him.

While there are many short-term benefits for children who respond well to medication, you may wonder about long-term benefits. Does treatment with medication make a difference in terms of adult adjustment? Because so many factors influence the adult outcome of the hyperactive child, this is a difficult question to answer. In general, however, young adults treated during childhood with stimulant medication have a more positive view of their childhood and seem to have less need for psychiatric treatment as adults. In addition, treatment with stimulant medication is also associated with:

- Less stealing in elementary school
- Fewer car accidents as adolescents and young adults
- Generally better social skills
- Higher self-esteem
- Fewer problems with aggression

Finally, it is important to point out that stimulant medication does *not* cease to be helpful during adolescence, as doctors used to believe. There is now convincing evidence that, during adolescence, hyperactive youngsters continue to benefit from stimulant medication. Hyperactive adults also benefit from stimulant treatment, although the percentage of those who improve is somewhat lower (about 50–60 percent). With Ritalin, the short duration of action is a problem for some, especially for the small minority for whom the drug's effects last only an hour or so. Because of its longer duration of action, Cylert might be a better choice for these individuals.

WHAT STIMULANT MEDICATION CANNOT DO

It is obvious from the above that stimulants may help your hyperactive child in many important ways. However, there are limits to what drugs can do for your child.

• They do not, for example, solve all social problems with other children. Although there is less friction, teasing, and fighting between the hyperactive child and his peers, these improvements are not always accompanied by increases in friendliness, helpfulness, and other positive social behavior. Special efforts may be needed to help the hyperactive child learn to make and keep friends (see Chapter 7).

• Pills are not a substitute for consistent parental discipline and guidance. While medication may help your child to be more agreeable and less argumentative, you may also benefit from professional help in developing more consistent methods of discipline.

• To date, behavioral scientists have not found evidence that stimulants result in long-term gains in academic achievement. In light of the fact that short-term gains in academic productivity and accuracy are reported, this may seem puzzling. Of course, medication cannot substitute for remedial help if your child is far behind academically or learning-disabled. Remember, too, that grades and achievement test results reflect homework as well as classwork. If your child takes stimulant medication only during school hours, he may have difficulty settling down to concentrate on homework after school, when the medication has worn off. Even if he does receive an afternoon dose, he may still go to great lengths to avoid homework. For such youngsters, a behavioral program can be helpful (see Chapter 8).

SIDE EFFECTS OF STIMULANT MEDICATION

In most cases, side effects of stimulant medication are mild and short-lived. They tend to occur at the beginning of treatment and, if they do not disappear after a few weeks, your doctor can usually control them by reducing the dose of medication. The medication can then be increased very gradually, as necessary, to a level which is most effective. (In fact, to minimize side effects at the start of treatment, many doctors begin with the lowest possible dose—5 milligrams of Ritalin, 5 milligrams of Dexedrine, or 18.75 milligrams of Cylert.)

The most common side effects are poor appetite and insomnia. About 60 percent of children treated with stimulants complain of some initial insomnia. Although fewer than 5 percent continue to have major difficulties for more than a month or so, doctors are often reluctant to prescribe a late-afternoon dose lest it interfere with sleep. This can be a serious problem for severely symptomatic children who must then attempt to cope with homework, chores, and other aspects of daily life without the benefit of medication for several critical hours each day.

The situation is even worse for a small minority of hyperactive children in whom there is such a marked deterioration in behavior as the medication wears off that the child is *worse than before taking the medication.* Authorities like Doctors Donald Klein and Rachel Gittelman,[13] both at Columbia University, and Dr. C. Keith Conners,[14] at Children's Hospital National Medical Center, now recommend that children who experience this "rebound" effect be given an additional dose of medication—often a smaller amount than that given earlier in the day—in the late afternoon or early evening. When this is done, these children are usually more settled and willing to retire at bedtime.

You may find that poor appetite is a more persistent problem for your child than insomnia. In most cases, although a weight loss of a few pounds may be observed, this is not a serious problem. You can reduce the appetite-suppressing effects of medication by giving the medication with, or immediately following, meals. If this is not possible, or if your child takes a long-acting form of medication, and you are worried about nutrition and weight loss, consider the use of a high-calorie snack before bedtime. Many families find that a milk-shake made by mixing a dietary supplement with the child's favorite ice cream is ideal for this purpose.

Headaches and stomachaches can also appear as side effects of medication. Again, these complaints tend to be short-lived and usually disappear if the dose is reduced slightly.

There have also been reports that some children treated with stimulants appear sad, tearful, and "touchy." According to Dr. Thomas Gualtieri, a well-known research psychiatrist at the University of North Carolina, these side effects are most likely to appear with Ritalin, especially at higher doses. Sometimes the child's mood improves when the dose is lowered. If not, however, Dr. Gualtieri urges that another medication be substituted immediately.

A question that has caused considerable controversy recently is whether stimulant medication can cause repetitive, involuntary motor movements called tics. There has even been speculation that stimulants can produce an irreversible neurological syndrome called Tourette's syndrome, a condition characterized by multiple, persistent motor and vocal tics. The most recent evidence does *not* support this notion. Rather, the apparent relationship between stimulant medication and Tourette's syndrome seems to be due to the fact that more than half of children with Tourette's syndrome are also hyperactive, with ADHD symptoms preceding the onset of tics by months or even years. These children may be treated with stimulants for ADHD, and months or years later, in the natural course of Tourette's syndrome, the tics emerge. This appears to be unrelated to the use of stimulants, which neither cause nor hasten the development of tics.

Another controversial issue is whether stimulants—especially Dexedrine—inhibit the child's physical growth, leading to short stature as an adult. A panel appointed by the U.S. Food and Drug Administration examined this question and concluded that, although there may be some suppression of growth during the first year or two of treatment, this is a transient problem. Children seem to develop a tolerance to this effect by about the third year of treatment, and any ultimate effects on adult height and weight appear to be minimal. Nevertheless, we do know that stimulant drugs do produce changes in levels of the hormones associated with growth. While these changes are not well understood at this time and the risk overall seems small, it is prudent to monitor the growth of children on these drugs and to give "drug holidays" when possible if growth seems affected, to minimize any possibility of long-term side effects.

A side effect which has been reported with Cylert, but not Dexedrine or Ritalin, is licking of the lips and light picking of the fingertips. Infrequently, skin rashes have also been reported. Neither side effect is dangerous, and both seem to respond to decreases in dosage. A more serious side effect is changes in liver function after several months of drug treatment. Although this reaction is rare, occurring only in 1–2 percent of children, it indicates hypersensitivity to the drug, and treatment with this drug must be discontinued immediately.

Are there differences in stimulant drugs in terms of side effects? Dexedrine appears to produce more severe side effects (especially appetite loss and growth suppression) than Ritalin or Cylert. There is also some evidence that Cylert may produce fewer side effects than Ritalin. Children vary tremendously in their response to these drugs, however, so it really depends on the individual child. Just because your child has side effects related to one stimulant does not necessarily mean that he will also have problems with side effects if another stimulant is used. In many cases in which reducing the dose has not been sufficient to reduce side effects to an acceptable level, switching to another medication has produced good results.

In addition to questions about the physical side effects of medication, you may worry about the possibility of psychological side effects. Some parents ask, "Won't he become dependent on medication?" Although "dependence" sounds frighteningly close to "addiction," it is important to repeat that there is *no* evidence that these children become addicted to, or abuse, their medication. Certainly, however, many hyperactive children must *rely* on medication to help them function well, just as a diabetic must rely on insulin or a person with severe allergies must rely on antihistamines.

You may also worry that taking medication will keep your child from facing his difficulties and learning to overcome them. Some parents have nightmare visions of a thirty-year-old who still cannot get dressed by himself in the morning or cope with other demands of daily life. Medication, we know, will not teach children specific skills, so many (if not most) hyperactive children will require additional types of treatment to improve their academic and social functioning.

MANAGING AND MONITORING MEDICATION

You might be surprised to learn that, when the right dose of medication is used, the effects can be observed almost immediately (within twenty to thirty minutes with Ritalin and Dexedrine). Unfortunately, because the dosage and timing of medication must be painstakingly established on an individual basis for each child, it is often the case that the hyperactive child does not receive an appropriate dose of medication.

According to Dr. Paul Wender, a psychiatrist who has written many excellent books and articles on the subject of ADHD, "The most common failure in . . . treatment (with stimulant medication) results from the use of inadequate amounts of medication for too short a period of time. It has been fairly common in my experience to see children who had received insufficient doses referred to as 'unresponsive' . . . they responded satisfactorily when given adequate amounts of medication."[15]

The question of the most appropriate dose of stimulant medication has been the focus of much research and debate. At this time, there seems to be general agreement on the guidelines presented in Figure 7, although Dr. Alan Zametkin cautions that these guidelines are not "carved in stone" and that every child's responses *must* be considered individually.

A related problem concerns the timing of each dose of medication during the day. Ritalin and Dexedrine are short-acting. In the majority of children, the effects will last for a maximum of three to four hours, although a few children may show benefit for up to six hours and a few will benefit for only about two hours. Therefore, although some children with very mild symptoms might be helped by a single morning dose of medication (especially if they have most of their academic subjects during the morning), most hyperactive children will need two or even three daily doses of Ritalin or Dexedrine for maximum benefit throughout the day.

If there are problems determining when the medication wears off, an hourly monitoring system can provide valuable information. To use this system, the parent or teacher identifies a list of problem behavior and uses a chart (see Figure 8) to record occurrences of these such as "out of seat," "off task," "fights with brother," and so on.

The chart is kept handy, and, when misbehavior occurs, a mark is made in the appropriate time column. Over a period of several days, this yields a picture of the child's typical behavior throughout the day, so trouble spots can be easily identified. Although this technique appears cumbersome, it is actually quite simple for even the busiest parent or teacher to use, and the information obtained is well worth the little bit of effort involved.

DRUG	DOSE RANGE (SINGLE DOSE)	DOSES PER DAY	STARTING DOSE AND TITRATION
Ritalin (methylphenidate)	0.3–1 mg/kg	1–3	Starting dose 5 mg. Increase each dose by 5 mg every three to five days until benefit is obtained or side effects occur. Single doses over 20 mg are seldom beneficial. One 20-mg sustained-release tablet is equivalent to two 10-mg doses, four hours apart.
Dexedrine (dextroamphetamine)	0.15–0.5 mg/kg	1–3	Starting dose 2.5 mg (ages three to five); 5 mg (ages six and up). Increase each dose by 2.5 mg every three to five days until benefit is obtained or side effects occur. One 5-mg spansule is equivalent to two 5-mg doses, four hours apart.
Cylert (pemoline)	0.5–3 mg/kg	1	Starting dose 18.75 mg. Increase daily dose to 3 mg/kg over a period of one week to ten days.

Figure 7. Stimulant drug dosage and titration.

Problem Behavior

1. _____
2. _____
3. _____
4. _____
5. _____

Name _____

DATE	7–8	8–9	9–10	10–11	11–12	12–1	1–2	2–3	3–4	4–5	5–6	6–7	7–8	8–9	9–10	10–11

Figure 8. Hourly monitoring form.

Ritalin and Dexedrine are both available in long-acting forms (Ritalin sustained-release, Dexedrine spansules). Unfortunately, although some children seem to respond well, the long-acting forms do not give consistent results throughout the day for all children. Again, an hourly monitoring procedure is helpful in determining whether or not a child responds well to this form of medication.

If your child does not show improvement by the time the maximum single dose is reached, or if side effects prevent further increases before an effective dose is reached, the medication should be discontinued and a different stimulant used. *You should not assume that your child's failure to respond positively to one stimulant means that he will not respond to another:* it is estimated that 20–50 percent of children who do poorly on one stimulant drug respond quite well to the use of another.

Dr. Russell Barkley recommends that the first medication used be Ritalin. He adds that Cylert is usually ineffective with children younger than the age of five, as are Ritalin and Dexedrine in children under the age of three. Children's responses to stimulant medication change with age, so a child who failed to respond at the age of four or five may respond well a year or two later.

In some children who do well initially on medication, a mild tolerance may develop after a month or two and symptoms may reappear. For most of these children, a slight increase in dosage usually corrects this, with no further increases in dose required. Unfortunately, some children continue to develop tolerance at higher doses. For these children, stimulant medication is not helpful and another kind of medication, such as an antidepressant, should be substituted.

Whether medication is given before or after meals seems to make little difference in terms of effectiveness (but, as noted, giving medication after meals may help the child with appetite problems). However, Dexedrine should not be taken with orange juice because acidifying agents such as ascorbic acid interfere with the body's ability to absorb the drug.

Can stimulants be used with other medications? Generally, the answer is a qualified yes, but you should always inform any physician treating your child that the child is taking stimulant medication, especially if another medication is prescribed. Stimulants have been used safely in treating hyperactive children who are also taking medication for epilepsy. However, stimulants can raise blood levels of anticonvulsants, so great care is needed in establishing correct doses of both medications if they are taken at the same time. There have also been reports that, in at least some children, medications containing antihistamines can block the action of stimulants and render them ineffective.

Dr. Mina Dulcan, a child psychiatrist on the faculty at the University of Pittsburgh, suggests that parents also follow these guidelines for children on stimulant medication:[16]

• Your child should have a drug-free period of two weeks or so* during the school year—preferably in the late winter or early spring, by which time he is well known to his teachers— to determine whether medication is still required. Summer drug holidays of two to four weeks are also desirable to minimize possible effects on growth, especially if your child is taking Dexedrine.

• Do not make your child responsible for taking his own medication. He is likely to forget or, in the case of children who object to taking medication, throw the pills in the trash. Also, your child may not appreciate being asked "Did you take your pill?" at the first sign of misbehavior. This can be avoided if you dispense the medication.

• Have your child's height and weight checked at least twice a year. If your child is short, this should be done every three months.

• Be sure that there is adequate communication between your child's teachers and his doctor and that the doctor re-

---

* If it becomes clear within a day or two that the child's behavior deteriorates without medication, the medication can be reinstated immediately.

ceives regular reports from school. This is especially important when adjusting medication or undertaking drug-free trials. (You can help by providing written permission for your doctor and your child's teachers to communicate with each other concerning your child. Include all names and telephone numbers to make communicating easier for everyone involved.

YOUR CHILD'S CONCERNS

What should you tell your child about a trial of stimulant medication? Some doctors advocate a policy of "full disclosure," while others recommend that the child simply be told, "I want you to take this medication." It is my policy to explain the use of medication as fully as possible, using the analogy of fuel for a car (see Chapter 3). Most children readily accept this explanation and agree to a trial of medication.

With older children and adolescents, however, you may encounter considerable resistance to the idea of taking medication. Sometimes children's objections stem from dislike of side effects such as appetite suppression, a "druggy" feeling, or feelings of sadness and listlessness. If this is the case, your doctor should immediately lower the dose or switch to a different stimulant.

Your child's initial objections may diminish as he comes to appreciate that medication is helpful to him, but this certainly is not always the case. In fact, objections are likely to increase with age and length of time on medication, and, in spite of benefits which are obvious to everyone else, the child may insist that the medication is not helpful and that he does not need it. This can be baffling and frustrating, and you might be tempted into lengthy debates to try to persuade the child of the need for medication. Such debates are usually fruitless, however, because some hyperactive children really cannot detect changes in their own behavior and so cannot appreciate the benefits of medication. Or your child may fear drug abuse and object to medication on that basis. Other objections (which may not always be voiced openly) often center around fear of being humiliated by other children and stigmatized as "different," "weird," or "crazy." For the teenager, in particular, taking medication may mean an acknowledgment that he is defective in some way and that he is not in complete control of his own behavior.

The following comments by hyperactive teenagers and young adults treated with stimulant medication illustrate these feelings:[17,18]

"Taking it meant I was dumb."

"I felt rotten about having to take pills; why me? I had no insight into why."

"Kids at school laughed at me for having to take pills."

"I felt embarrassed in front of other kids and in the family."

As parents, how can you help a child with these concerns? The first step, of course, is to listen to the child's point of view. Don't argue with the child or point out how much his behavior improves with medication. When you are sure that you understand the child's objections, try to solve the problem with him: "Let's put our heads together and see if we can come up with some good solutions to the problem."

Parents who are sensitive to their child's fear of embarrassment will make every effort to spare him humiliation about his medication. This means that medication will not be used to shame a child when he is having a bad day, nor will his medication be discussed in front of other people. If your child takes medication during school hours, he may worry that his classmates will notice and ask embarrassing questions. (Some children get around this problem by telling their classmates that the medication is allergy medication or vitamins.) It can be difficult to devise unobtrusive ways for the child to receive his medication, especially since the child himself usually cannot reliably remember to take his medication or go to the nurse's office. A wristwatch with an alarm can sometimes be helpful in such cases. Under no circumstances should the child be reminded in front of the class or have his name called over the public address system!

If your child objects to taking medication, you may be tempted to allow the child to discontinue medication "to see if he can do it on his own." Except for the annual drug-free period used to check a child's continued need for medication, I do not agree with this practice: in most cases, it amounts to setting a child up to fail. Whenever possible, I recommend that parents remain firm in their stance that medication must be taken exactly as prescribed.

OTHER MEDICATIONS USED TO TREAT ADHD

TRICYCLIC ANTIDEPRESSANTS

In 1960 tricyclic antidepressants were found to be helpful in treating bed wetting. Not long afterward, reports began to appear concerning their beneficial effects on symptoms of hyperactivity. Like stimulant medication, tricyclics are believed to work by acting on neurotransmitters in the brain.

Of the wide variety of drugs other than stimulants that have been tried in the treatment of ADHD, the tricyclics imipramine and desipramine have been the most carefully studied. In general, they seem to be nearly as effective as stimulants in many children. In addition, their effects are longer lasting than those of the stimulants, so there is better control of symptoms during the late afternoon and evening, without insomnia. They also appear to have a weak but positive effect on mood and poor self-image, neither of which is helped by stimulant medication. Unfortunately, although the effects of the tricyclics can sometimes be seen as early as a day or two after starting treatment, some children develop tolerance to the medication after several weeks or months and no longer derive a benefit from them.

Because these drugs can be so helpful for some hyperactive children who do not respond to stimulants, it is unfortunate that there are still some unresolved questions about them and that definite guidelines for their use have not been more clearly established. Although some children respond immediately to fairly low doses (50–100 milligrams), others require doses of up to 5 milligrams per kilogram of body weight before improvement occurs.

At lower doses, side effects are not usually a problem with the tricyclics. At doses higher than 100 milligrams or so, some children may have dry mouth, drowsiness, constipation, or blurred vision. Typically, these side effects are only mildly annoying, but a few children do find them too unpleasant and medication must be stopped.

Desipramine is less likely than imipramine to produce these side effects. According to Dr. C. Thomas Gualtieri, it is also less likely to impair fine motor coordination and memory, effects sometimes seen with imipramine. Although these effects are small, they may be significant with hyperactive children, many of whom already have problems in these areas. For these reasons, Dr. Gualtieri recommends that desipramine be used instead of imipramine.

Certain precautions must be observed if tricyclic antidepressants are prescribed for children. Like other medications, they must be kept securely beyond the reach of younger children because an overdose can be fatal. Heart rate and blood pressure should be monitored routinely, and EKG monitoring should also be done routinely. This is especially important at higher doses. Finally, these medications should be given in divided doses (two doses a day) instead of a single daily dose.

Despite their potential dangers, experts consider tricyclic antidepressants a valuable "second line" of treatment for ADHD. According to Dr. Michael Rancurello, medical director of the Child Psychiatric Treatment Service Inpatient Unit at Western Psychiatric Institute in Pittsburgh, "Tricyclics seem to represent a rational treatment alternative in the event that stimulants are either ineffective or contraindicated . . . [or for] those in whom sleep disturbance, severe late afternoon symptom escape, or . . . irritability, [or] dysphoria cannot be managed by stimulant dose reduction, the addition of a late afternoon dose, or changing to another stimulant."[19]

Dr. Rancurello reminds us, however, that if tricyclic medication is stopped, it should be withdrawn slowly, over a period of two weeks or more, to avoid the possibility of uncomfortable flulike symptoms, which can occur if the medication is stopped abruptly.

MONOAMINE OXIDASE INHIBITORS

Monoamine oxidase inhibitors (MAOIs) such as clorgyline and tranylcypromine are another class of drugs commonly used to treat depression in adults. Studies conducted by Doctors Judith Rapoport and Alan Zametkin at the National Institute of Mental Health have shown that these drugs produce immediate and clear-cut reductions in hyperactive, impulsive behavior and that the effects cannot be distinguished from the effects of stimulants. In spite of these excellent results, Dr. Rapoport notes that MAOIs "will never find a major use" with hyperactive children because dangerous reactions can occur if the child violates rigid dietary restrictions or takes any medication containing a stimulant (found in many over-the-counter medications).

However, MAOIs can be used with hyperactive adults because most adults can be trusted to follow the dietary restrictions. Dr. Paul Wender[20] found that low doses (20–30 milligrams a day) of the MAOI pargyline improved mood, attention span, anger, hyperactivity, and disorganization in hyperactive adults. Dr. Wender also reported similar results with the MAOI L-deprenyl, which appears to produce fewer side effects than pargyline. Both drugs have the advantage of twenty-four-hour effectiveness. The MAOIs appear to be particularly helpful to hyperactive adults who complain of frequent low mood.

ANTIPSYCHOTIC DRUGS

Sometimes referred to as "major tranquilizers," this group of drugs includes the phenothiazines (Thorazine, Mellaril) and halperidol (Haldol). These drugs are most commonly used to treat severe psychiatric disorders like schizophrenia.

Antipsychotic drugs are generally less effective than stimulants in treating ADHD. Although they reduce activity and impulsiveness, they do not improve attention or learning (in fact, the phenothiazines can actually interfere with learning and attention). Antipsychotic drugs also have serious side effects such as drowsiness, weight gain, and sensitivity of the skin to sunlight. With higher doses and long-term use, there is the possibility that involuntary motor movements can develop.

For these reasons, antipsychotic drugs have been used less and less in recent years to treat ADHD. In fact, as Dr. Gualtieri states, it is extremely unlikely that these drugs will be prescribed for children very much longer. Certainly, their use should be considered only when symptoms are severe and when all other measures have failed.

OTHER PHYSICAL APPROACHES TO TREATMENT

DIETARY MANAGEMENT

Additive-free (Defined) Diets. Since 1975, when Dr. Benjamin Feingold published a book called *Why Your Child is Hyperactive,* there has been a tremendous amount of controversy surrounding his theory that food additives such as dyes and preservatives are responsible for hyperactive symptoms in many children. Dr. Feingold's theory has commonsense appeal, and, because it appeared at a time of increasing public concern about toxic substances and pollutants in the environment, it received widespread media coverage. The Feingold Diet, free of additives, preservatives, and salicylates, was welcomed enthusiastically by parents seeking a "natural" approach to managing ADHD, and there have been many reports of dramatic behavioral improvements resulting from the diet. Dr. Feingold himself claims that over half of the children treated with his diet show significant improvement.

When these claims were subjected to close scientific scrutiny, however, results fell far short of expectations. Observing groups of hyperactive children who alternated between additive-free diets and normal diets, researchers could detect diet-related improvements in only a small proportion of the children. Even in these children, improvement was not consistently reported by parents, teachers, and other observers.

In January 1982 the National Institutes of Health held a three-day conference on controlled diets and ADHD. At this conference, experts presented evidence on the subject to a panel composed of biomedical researchers, practicing physicians, consumers, and representatives of health advocacy groups. The panel's task was to assess the evidence and come to some conclusions about the effectiveness of defined diets in the management of ADHD.

The panel concluded that there may be some hyperactive children who respond to controlled diets. This group, however, is probably quite small, and results may be much less impressive than previous reports indicated. The panel also cautioned, "Defined diets should not be universally used in the treatment of childhood hyperactivity at this time" and "A defined diet should not be initiated until thorough and appropriate evaluation of the children and their families and full consideration of all traditional therapeutic options . . . have taken place."

Obviously, I cannot recommend the Feingold Diet or any of the defined diets as likely to be helpful to your hyperactive child. These diets are complicated and time-consuming to use and difficult to enforce, especially if your child is away for many hours every day. More important, you may do your child a real disservice if you focus on diet to the exclusion of more effective treatment methods.

Sugar-Free Diets. You may also be curious about the (supposed) relationship between refined sugar and hyperactive, impulsive behavior. Many parents are certain that their child's behavior worsens when he eats food high in sugar.

This is, however, another case in which there is a great discrepancy between anecdotal reports and the results of careful laboratory studies. Dr. Richard Milich, a psychologist at the University of Kentucky, has conducted a series of painstaking investigations into the effects of sugar on the behavior of hyperactive children. Dr. Milich examined the effects of sugar on 30 different aspects of child behavior, including academic productivity and accuracy, social behavior, on-task behavior, and body movement. His results, he states, provide "absolutely no suggestion that sugar adversely affects the performance of hyperactive children."[21]

Why, then, do parents so often report a worsening of behavior around Halloween, Easter, and Christmas, holidays traditionally associated with a high consumption of candy and other sugary foods? Perhaps it is because holidays are also associated with parties, visiting friends and relatives, changes in routine, and a lot of bustle and excitement. Under these circumstances, the hyperactive child is likely to become overstimulated and lose control of his behavior. Thus, while sugar may seem to be the culprit, other factors may actually be responsible for a worsening in your child's behavior.

General Nutrition. Although researchers have come up with very little evidence supporting defined and sugar-free diets, this does *not* mean that general nutrition does not play a role in child behavior. Research is quite clear in showing that a good breakfast, for example, is particularly important for children. Children who miss breakfast perform poorly on a variety of different tests when these tests are given in the morning. For the hyperactive child, then, who needs every advantage we can give him, a good breakfast is a very good idea.

Caffeine. Caffeine, a mild central nervous system stimulant, is found in some of the foods that children commonly consume, such as tea, chocolate, and cola beverages. Because caffeine increases alertness and attention, there has been some interest in its effects on the behavior of hyperactive children. At least ten studies of caffeine treatment of ADHD have appeared since 1973. Of these, nine have failed to find any beneficial effects of caffeine on hyperactive behavior. This certainly suggests that caffeine is not an effective approach to alleviating the symptoms of ADHD.

5

What Else Can We Do?

Psychological Methods of Treatment

PSYCHOTHERAPY

WHAT IS PSYCHOTHERAPY?

For many years—and even today, in some professional circles
—psychologists and psychiatrists considered psychotherapy
the treatment of choice for dealing with disordered behavior
and emotions in both children and adults. Sometimes called
"the talking cure," the term "psychotherapy" encompasses a
wide variety of methods and techniques aimed at helping
people make changes in attitudes, emotions, and behavior
patterns. Although there are many "schools" of psychotherapy, most traditional forms are based on the assumption that
abnormal behavior is caused by underlying psychological
problems. Psychotherapy attempts to deal with these underlying problems—the unconscious conflicts, fears, anxieties, and
fantasies—that interfere with the patient's ability to cope with
the demands of everyday life.

Depending what school the psychotherapist belongs to, he or she uses certain techniques to help the patient gain insight into the nature of his difficulties. The specific techniques vary: *play therapists,* for example, use play materials, games, and toys to build a working relationship with the child and to help them understand the child's fears, needs, and inner turmoil. In *group therapy,* the child is helped to see what effects he has on others and how his own behavior causes problems for him. The group serves as a safe place in which the child can work on these problems and try out new, more satisfying ways of behaving. In *family therapy,* the child's difficulties are seen as the result of conflict among family members. The focus of treatment is usually the entire family, and the family therapist tries to change the patterns of communication among all family members.

DOES PSYCHOTHERAPY HELP HYPERACTIVE CHILDREN?

Many people assume that psychotherapy is superior to medication as a treatment for ADHD because psychotherapy gets at the supposed source of the problem (disturbed emotions), while medication treats only the symptoms. Since, however, current evidence indicates that the hyperactive child's difficulties are caused by physical malfunctions in the brain, it makes little sense to look to psychological methods for relief. And, in fact, there is simply no convincing evidence that psychotherapy helps to alleviate the hyperactive child's inattentiveness, poor impulse control, or motor hyperactivity.

This does not mean that psychological intervention has nothing to offer the hyperactive child and his family. On this issue, I agree with Dr. Paul Wender's conclusion that *"some* forms of psychological intervention are useful with *some* [hyperactive] children *some* of the time."[22]

Family therapy, for example, may be useful in identifying any misunderstandings which exist among family members. Family therapy can also help parents work together to manage a child's problem behavior more effectively. In addition, treatment sessions involving both parents and children can provide a forum in which the concerns of all family members can be addressed and compromises negotiated.

Psychological intervention with the child himself may be beneficial if it helps him understand the nature of his difficulties and how he can learn to cope with what amounts to a chronic condition. It can also help the child deal with problems that often go hand in hand with ADHD, such as poor self-esteem.

The socially isolated child or the child who feels that ADHD means he is weird, different, or defective may also benefit from group therapy with other hyperactive children who are close to him in age. Sadly, such specialized groups are very difficult to find. This is unfortunate because frank discussions in which the children air their feelings and concerns can help the hyperactive child see that he is not the only one in the world with this problem. Meeting other hyperactive children who take medication for their condition may be particularly helpful for children who object to taking medication. Talking about their common concerns often forms the basis for friendships among the children, and receiving acceptance and support from others can be very gratifying to a child who has come to view himself as an oddball and a social outcast.

COGNITIVE TRAINING

After many years of research on the problems of hyperactive children, Canadian psychologist Dr. Virginia Douglas concluded that activity level was *not* the fundamental cause of their difficulties. Instead, she found that their difficulties stemmed from their inability to sustain attention and their poor impulse control. As she put it, "These youngsters are apparently unable to keep their own impulses under control in order to cope with situations in which care, concentrated attention, or organized planning are required. They tend to react with the first idea that occurs to them. . . . I have come to think of (their problem) as the inability to 'stop, look and listen' . . ."[23]

Other researchers agreed with Dr. Douglas. A short attention span became recognized as a "core" problem, and the name of the disorder itself was changed to Attention-deficit Hyperactivity Disorder to reflect this change in thinking. Dr. Douglas's findings also stimulated considerable interest in developing methods to teach hyperactive children to control their impulsive behavior by planning ahead, stopping to think, and carefully following a plan and correcting any errors.

Beginning in the early 1970s, a number of "cognitive training" programs were designed to teach these skills to hyperactive children. These programs emphasized teaching the hyperactive child to approach a task or problem analytically by asking himself such questions as "What is my problem?" and "What is it I have to do?" As a second step, the child would be instructed to think ahead and develop a plan by asking himself, "How can I do this?" To help prevent impulsive actions, the child might be encouraged to come up with alternative plans for solving the problem or completing the task, then to evaluate the relative merits of each plan and select the best one. These programs also taught children to evaluate their own performance while working on the task and to check frequently to be sure they were following the plan they had developed by asking "How am I doing?" and "Am I following my plan?" Because hyperactive children often make careless errors, these cognitive training programs also stressed carefully checking work and correcting any errors.

After initial training on such tasks as puzzles, mazes, and copying designs, most training programs taught children to apply their new skills to schoolwork and social situations. For example, to help children learn to cope with difficult social situations in a less impulsive fashion, training programs include role playing, training in social problem-solving skills, and exercises to teach cooperation with others.

Researchers in the United States and Canada developed and tested several cognitive training programs, some of them quite elaborate—and rather expensive. At the University of Illinois at Chicago, for example, under the direction of Dr. Ronald Brown, one-hour training sessions were held twice weekly for three months.[24] A program in New York, under the direction of Doctors Howard Abikoff, from the Long Island Jewish–Hillside Medical Center, and Rachel Gittelman, from Columbia University provided two hours of training weekly for four months.[25] If these services were provided by a child psychologist in private practice, parents could expect to pay anywhere from $1,000 to $2,000 or even more.

On the face of it, cognitive training would certainly seem to be a very promising approach to the problems of the hyperactive child. Unfortunately, it doesn't seem to work very well, according to some of those who have been most involved in developing and testing cognitive training programs for hyperactive children. After ten years of research, "the results are very discouraging," concludes Dr. Abikoff. At the conclusion of their sixteen-week cognitive training program for fifty hyperactive youngsters, Doctors Abikoff and Gittelman found that cognitive training did *not* reduce the children's need for stimulant medication, nor did it result in improved classroom behavior or gains in academic productivity or achievement. Social behavior was similarly unaffected, despite eight weeks of training specifically devoted to teaching the children how to resolve social problems. In fact, Doctors Abikoff and Gittelman describe an incident in their program which vividly illustrates this lack of improvement: "Three youngsters had worked remarkably well together on a cooperative exercise. They left for home together in a taxi, to be brought back only minutes later. The taxi driver refused to ride with the children because of the fighting that had immediately erupted over who would get the two window seats. The driver's reported efforts to control the boys were unsuccessful."[26]

In other large, well-designed cognitive training programs

with hyperactive youngsters, such as Dr. Brown's program at the University of Illinois at Chicago, researchers have also come up empty-handed. At this point, the evidence regarding cognitive training seems clear: the results are, indeed, very discouraging.

BEHAVIOR MODIFICATION

DOES BEHAVIOR MODIFICATION HELP HYPERACTIVE CHILDREN?

Psychologists were at first particularly enthusiastic about behavior modification because they hoped to produce a non-medical treatment for ADHD that would equal or surpass the effectiveness of stimulant medication without the side effects of medication. Unfortunately, this hope has *not* been fully realized. In fact, the reverse actually appears to be true: surveying the results of scientific studies, Dr. Gittelman concluded that medication is more effective than behavior modification for hyperactive children.

Researchers have discovered, however, that some children who are only partially improved on stimulant medication can benefit from a combination of medication and behavior modification. For many of these children, combined treatment is necessary to bring about more appropriate behavior. Behavior modification also appears to offer an alternative for children who, for one reason or another, cannot take medication. The results, however, are apt to be less dramatic than those obtained with medication.

Behavior modification does not offer a cure for ADHD. Like stimulant medication, it is a means of managing the problem and, like medication, the effects do not last if the treatment is stopped. Another point to bear in mind is that a behavior modification program can involve a great deal of effort and energy on the part of parents and teachers. Thus, it is far more expensive than medication and may not be suitable for all families with hyperactive children.

If you decide to undertake a behavior modification program with your child, it's a good idea to consult a mental health professional with special expertise in this area. Although the guidelines in the next section can give you a general sense of direction, behavior modification is actually a very sophisticated technology, and a behavior modification program has the best chance of succeeding if it is used under the guidance of a skilled professional.

How Behavior Modification Works

Behavior modification is based on the idea that specific behaviors are learned because they produce specific effects. In other words, people (and animals) learn to do many of the things they do because of the consequences that follow their actions. Behavior is affected most strongly by consequences which immediately follow the behavior. When there is a delay between a particular behavior (such as overeating) and the consequences that follow (weight gain), the consequences are not likely have a very pronounced effect on the behavior.

In general, consequences that are enjoyable or rewarding tend to strengthen behavior, making it more likely that the behavior will occur again. Thus, a puppy who is rewarded with a pat and a biscuit learns to come when he is called, and a toddler learns to say "please" if this behavior results in a cookie. Similarly, we turn up the thermostat on chilly days because we have learned that this action produces the welcome sensation of warmth.

When there is no payoff for a behavior, the behavior tends to weaken and eventually stop altogether. You would not keep putting coins in a candy machine that did not reward your behavior with a candy bar, nor would you long continue to wave and smile at a neighbor who did not return your greeting. You would cease your efforts even more abruptly if, instead of an absence of positive consequences, you encountered consequences which were unpleasant or painful—if you received a shock when you deposited a coin in the vending machine, for example, or if your neighbor threw a rock in response to your greeting.

Consequences need not be dramatic in order to have an effect on behavior, nor are they always immediately apparent to an observer. A smile or a wink can be a very effective positive consequence; a frown or a menacing glare can serve as a negative consequence, bringing a particular behavior to an abrupt halt. We often underestimate the power of such "social" consequences, but they can be surprisingly effective in strengthening or weakening behavior.

Part of the power of social consequences—indeed, *all* consequences which follow behavior—lies in the information they convey to the person who receives them. Although we tend to focus on the pleasure-or-pain aspects of positive and negative consequences, consequences also provide people with essential information about their own behavior. Positive consequences tell us that our behavior is appropriate or "on the right track," just as route markers and road signs along the highway tell the motorist he is going in the right direction. Conversely, negative consequences signal an error and tell us to change direction. (An important point to note here about negative consequences is that they only tell us what *doesn't* work: they don't provide any information about what we should do instead.)

To emphasize the informational properties of positive consequences, I prefer to use the technical term "reinforcer" instead of the term "reward." Because "reward" implies something out of the ordinary, a special treat for special effort, it is difficult to think in terms of "rewarding" everyday behavior. Such an approach seems strange and artificial to many parents. Some object to what they consider bribery. Others ask, "Why should I reward him for doing what he's supposed to do?" and "Isn't this going to cost me a fortune?"

The term "reinforcement" carries no such connotations,

calls up no visions of daily trips to the toy store and McDonald's. To reinforce simply means to strengthen, and the best way to strengthen certain behaviors is to be sure that positive consequences follow the behavior. Cast in this light, providing reinforcements for behavior doesn't seem like such a strange idea, after all. In fact, it makes very good sense.

USING POSITIVE CONSEQUENCES

Positive consequences, or reinforcers, are the most potent tool in a good behavior management program. How carefully you select and use reinforcers will determine the success of your program. You must, for example, use reinforcers that are meaningful to your child. Like adults, children have their idiosyncracies. What one child considers a treat, another might dread. As a parent, you are in the best position to know what your child most values and enjoys.

What Can You Use? Reinforcers need not be elaborate. In fact, the simpler, the better. Many of the common, everyday activities your child now takes for granted—watching television, playing outside, talking on the telephone, riding his bike, playing computer games—can be incorporated easily into a behavior management program. To a great extent, successful use of these reinforcers depends on how you present them. It is much more effective to say, for example, "When you finish your homework, you may go out to play" instead of "You can't go out to play if you don't finish your homework."

Here are some other tips to keep in mind when selecting reinforcers:

• *Avoid the "goodies trap."* Relying on toys and treats is artificial and expensive. Instead of buying a lot of special things, use things you would ordinarily purchase for the child and let him earn them. With some material goods, you can get maximum mileage with a "rental" arrangement. This means that you purchase the item and let the child earn the privilege of using it on a daily or weekly basis. For example, instead of promising, "We'll get you a stereo if you make good grades this semester," buy the stereo and let the child rent it on a week-to-week basis. If grades and homework are satisfactory for the week, the child earns the use of the stereo the following week; if not, the stereo is removed from his room for a week. This strategy allows you to occasionally provide your child with a coveted but expensive item without bankrupting you. It also avoids long delays between the good behavior and the reinforcer, during which the hyperactive child is apt to become discouraged and give up.

• *Vary the reinforcers.* Think about your favorite food. Now think about having it at every meal, day in and day out, for a month. Ugh! Even the things we love best begin to cloy if we indulge in them too much, a point which may be especially important with hyperactive children. Dr. Russell Barkley thinks it is possible that hyperactive children tend to tire of things and become bored more quickly than other children. As one example, he cites the fact that, when hyperactive children are provided with a variety of toys and left to play on their own, they change toys much more frequently than other children do. In fact, they spend only about half as much time with each toy, in comparison with other youngsters.

• *Use lots of praise.* Remember that "social reinforcers" such as praise and attention provide an excellent source of positive feedback. Smiles, winks, and hugs don't cost you a penny. They are easy to use, can be delivered on the spot, and you have an endless supply. No child has ever suffered ill effects from too much praise for good behavior!

Although we all enjoy receiving praise for our efforts, most of us are surprisingly stingy when it comes to dispensing it to others. On the other hand, we tend to be quite generous with criticism. In fact, as Dr. Barkley's research reminds us, parents of hyperactive children tend to rely very heavily on criticism and negative feedback with their hyperactive children. This is understandable—hyperactive children seem to do so much that calls forth criticism and so little that is praiseworthy—but it is unfortunate and inefficient. Nagging and criticism not only do nothing to improve the child's self-concept or the relationship between parent and child; negative feedback conveys less information to the child because it tells him only what he should not do. It does not suggest what he should do instead.

Try this little experiment. Make two columns on an index card, one marked "Praise" and the other marked "Criticism." Carry the card with you for three days and make a check in the appropriate column each time you praise or criticize your child for something he is doing. The results are likely to be an eye-opener. If you are passing out much more criticism than praise, try a little behavior modification on yourself. From your index card, estimate the number of times per day that you compliment your child on something he is doing. Try to increase this by two or three times each day. To remind yourself of your goal and to provide feedback on your progress, put the appropriate number of beans or pennies in one pocket. Each time you give your child positive feedback, transfer one token to the other pocket. If you do this faithfully for a couple of weeks, you can begin to break the habit of providing too much criticism and too little praise.

In addition to direct praise from you, an overheard compliment can give a big boost to good behavior. Let your child "accidentally" overhear you bragging about his good behavior to your spouse, a neighbor, or another family member. Be specific so the child knows exactly what he's done well. "Pat's been so good lately," conveys no useful information to the child. On the other hand, "Pat made her bed this morning without a reminder," tells the child exactly what she did that met with your approval.

Parents sometimes report that their child doesn't like praise; that it embarrasses him. If your child acts indifferent to praise from you, it may mean that he is so used to receiving criticism that he simply tunes out most of what you say, good and bad. If he seems annoyed or embarrassed when you compliment him, this is your signal to praise the job, not the child. For example, try "Good job cleaning the kitchen, Seth," instead of "Seth, you're such a big help to me." If Seth objects that he really didn't do such a good job, don't press the point. Smile and ignore the objections: they will soon cease.

Using Positive Consequences: Points to Remember. No matter how carefully you select reinforcers, they will do little good if you don't use them in the right manner. *Timing* is particularly critical. Since reinforcers are used to signal "That's right; keep it up," they are most effective when they follow hot on the heels of the behavior. A consequence that comes hours, days, or weeks later doesn't provide much useful feedback, especially for the hyperactive child. Hyperactive children, in particular, seem to have an unusually strong tendency to seek immediate reinforcement and are very susceptible to delays between behavior and reinforcement.

Other points to remember:

• *Be generous; reinforce often.* Scientists who have observed hyperactive children report that their overall performance improves considerably when reinforcers are delivered frequently. When reinforcers are few and far between, the performance of hyperactive children deteriorates more rapidly than the performance of other children—hyperactive children just seem to "fall apart" when they have to stick to a task for long periods without feedback.

If highway route markers were spaced a hundred miles apart, they would not be much help in guiding the traveler on his journey. Remember that reinforcers are behavioral "route markers." Use them frequently to help your child stay on the right road.

• *Reinforce small steps toward improvement.* Probably the single most common mistake parents make in using positive consequences is offering a huge payoff for a huge amount of improvement. Look at this example: "If you don't fight with your sister for a month, I'll buy you a new bike." The hyperactive youngster who seldom goes a day without a sibling battle has about as much chance of reaching this goal as he does of winning the lottery. A more reasonable plan is to offer smaller reinforcers for goals that are within the child's reach. If the child can occasionally make it through an entire day without an altercation with his sibling, the parent might give television privileges or a slightly later bedtime in exchange.

Think of a stairway with your goal at the top. You want your child to reach the top, but he cannot do it in a single leap: he must take it one step at a time. If the steps are too big, the goal too far away, he will fail and become discouraged. Plan small steps to insure success, and, as each step is mastered, move to the next.

• *Keep the horse in front of the cart: don't reinforce what hasn't actually happened.* Another common mistake parents make is reinforcing a behavior before it occurs, instead of afterwards.

PARENT: "If I let you watch TV now, you have to promise that you'll do your chores later."
CHILD: "Sure, I promise."

Notice that what is being reinforced, or strengthened, in this example is not the desirable behavior (doing chores) but the behavior of making a promise. That's fine, if the child habitually honors his promises. Unfortunately, many hyperactive children are quick to make promises but woefully slow in following through on them.

You can avoid this dilemma by keeping in mind a simple, old-fashioned rule: "Work before you play."

USING NEGATIVE CONSEQUENCES

When parents are introduced to behavior modification, many are at first taken aback by the emphasis on positive consequences. This focus seems strange at first because it's the reverse of our usual disciplinary approach. When we think of managing and improving child behavior, we tend to think primarily in terms of putting a stop to problem behavior. Punishment is the first method that comes to mind. The idea of strengthening good behavior usually occurs only as an afterthought.

This is very unfortunate because punishment—especially the way in which it is often administered—is a very ineffective, inefficient way to manage child behavior. There are several problems with punishment:

• *Punishment conveys limited information.* The information that punishment carries is in some ways less useful than information conveyed by positive consequences. Remember that punishment only tells your child what he should not do; it does not suggest other alternatives. If you spank your child for teasing the dog, for example, he has to come up with another way to amuse himself. Of course, it's possible that, left to his own devices, he will turn to a more acceptable activity. It's equally likely, however—in fact, with a hyperactive child it is usually *more* than likely—that he will occupy himself with another unacceptable activity such as throwing rocks, cutting holes in the drapes, or pulling the tassels off his bedspread.

• *Punishment often results in power plays between parent and child.* A bad situation can escalate out of control if initial efforts to stop a problem through punishment fail and parents decide to increase the severity of the punishment. Spankings become beatings, stern lectures become screaming tirades, and privileges are taken away for months at a time. But the child can't give in or he'll lose face. Both parent and child are backed into corners. When this happens, neither can emerge the winner.

• *Punishment can backfire.* Psychologists know that punishment (especially physical punishment) sometimes produces effects quite different from those intended. In fact, punishment can actually lead to *increases* in undesirable behavior, especially tantrums and aggressiveness.

Despite these disadvantages, parents may continue to rely on punishment because they don't know what else to do.

Moreover, the tendency to punish is often strengthened by the fact that punishment can produce an immediate, if short-lived, change in behavior. This change is gratifying to the person who administers the punishment so the tendency to punish is reinforced.

Unless punishment is severe, however, it may not produce lasting changes in behavior. Think about it: how many times have you punished your child over and over for the same misbehavior—bouncing on the furniture, for example, or tormenting his sister? How many times have you turned around hours or even minutes later to find him busily engaged in the same pursuit, just as if you hadn't nagged, scolded, and swatted him a hundred times for this very activity?

Parents often report that they feel guilty about the amount of punishment they use to try to control their hyperactive child's behavior. The father of an eight-year-old boy said with some embarrassment, "It seems like we're on his case all the time. No wonder he doesn't like himself." Another parent admitted, "Our home is like a battlefield. Every day I promise myself that I'm going to be more patient; that we're going to make it through one whole day with no nagging or spanking. Then he does something like throwing rocks at the neighbor kids or writing on his bedroom walls and—boom!—there we go again."

It is obvious that there are many problems associated with using punishment to control the behavior of hyperactive children. Does this mean that you should abandon the use of punishment and rely strictly on positive consequences to manage your child's behavior? Absolutely not! That's not only unrealistic (real life is not all positive consequences); it wouldn't work, even if you could manage to do it. Studies of hyperactive children have shown that certain kinds of negative consequences are necessary to keep behavior on the right track: positive consequences alone are not enough.

It does mean, however, that you should probably make

changes in the way you think about and use punishment. In fact, I suggest that you begin by eliminating the word "punishment" from your vocabulary and even from your thinking. Replace it with the term "negative consequence" or "negative feedback." These terms help you remember that your role in managing your hyperactive child's behavior is that of a teacher or guide, rather than a police officer or a warden.

Negative Consequences: What Can You Use? Negative consequences do not have to be harsh or painful to be effective. Remember that the point is to steer the child away from bad behavior, not to hurt or humiliate him as traditional forms of punishment often do.

The method known as "Time Out" is an excellent example of a negative consequence that does not involve scolding, anger, or pain. Easy to use and surprisingly effective, this method has gained great popularity with parents and teachers. Time Out involves isolating the child in a boring place for a few minutes immediately after he misbehaves. Any boring place in the house will do nicely—a chair in the dining room, the back stairs—but you must be sure that it is, in fact, boring. For this reason, it's usually not effective to send a child to his room because he can simply occupy himself playing with his toys and books.

You might explain Time Out to your child as follows: "I know that you don't really want to do things that get you into trouble. But sometimes you goof and do something that makes us mad, like [examples specific to child]. When this happens, it tells me that you're not thinking about your behavior. To help you learn to think about your behavior, each time you goof, you will spend some time in a quiet spot thinking about what happened and how you could have done better. The quiet spot I'd like you to use is [specify a place of your choosing]. But, remember: you're supposed to be thinking, and to think you've got to be quiet. You can't think if you're hollering and yelling and asking how much time is left.

If that happens, I will set the timer back to the beginning and you'll have to start over again."

The length of time the child must spend in Time Out depends on the age of the child. With children under the age of five, three to five minutes will usually suffice. Use ten minutes for children between the ages of five and ten and fifteen to twenty minutes for children over the age of ten.

Remember that the child must "serve his time" in silence; otherwise, reset the timer and begin the Time Out period over again. Although some children will have to learn the hard way by spending lengthy periods of time in Time Out on the first couple of occasions—I know one four-year-old who spent *four hours* in Time Out the first time—most resistance will vanish if you remain firm and consistent. Resistance is lessened, too, if you label Time Out positively as a time for the child to think over his behavior instead of presenting it as punishment.

POOR: "You bad girl! Just for that, you have to go to Time Out. Get in there right now!"

GOOD: "Hitting your brother is against the rules. Please go into Time Out for ten minutes and think about what you might have done instead."

You can also use Time Out if your child misbehaves when you are away from home. It's a little cumbersome but it can be done, either by using your car, a restroom, or a quiet corner as a Time Out spot or by informing the child that he will have to spend time in Time Out as soon as you return home. Although this doesn't have the immediacy of Time Out used at home, nor does it provide a few minutes apart for both you and your child to cool off, it is still a useful approach.

You might also want to use *penalties* as negative consequences for unacceptable behavior. This is the time-honored practice of removing a privilege when the child misbehaves. If this doesn't seem to work effectively with your child, you may have overlooked some of the finer points of this method. If, for example, you have used very long-term penalties or removed virtually all of the child's privileges, he may have decided, "What's the use? I might as well do what I want: I've got nothing else to lose." Another problem with long-term penalties is that parents often relent after a period of good behavior or if a special occasion comes up. As a rule of thumb, a penalty should be in effect no longer than one day, at most, for every five years of the child's age. Longer penalties are not more effective: they are only more difficult to enforce.

When possible, the penalty should have some logical relationship to the undesirable behavior.

POOR: Lisa leaves her bike in the driveway for the third time in a week. You tell her that she may not have dessert as a result of her forgetfulness.

GOOD: Lisa leaves her bike in the driveway again. You tell her that she may not ride her bike for forty-eight hours so that she will remember to put it away the next time.

As an alternative to removing privileges, you might want to consider a *work penalty* for misbehavior, especially if the child's behavior caused inconvenience or expense to another person. Some good work penalties include an hour of weeding the garden, scrubbing the kitchen floor, washing the car, or cleaning the bathrooms. Work penalties do involve more effort on your part than simply taking away a privilege because it is likely that you will have to supervise the child's work rather closely. They have the advantage, however, of allowing the child to make restitution for his misbehavior and wipe the slate clean.

Nine-year-old Alan arrived home from the playground almost an hour late—again. His mother told him that she had been worried about him, unable to attend to her work, and had even driven around the neighborhood looking for him. "Since you took up so much of my time and caused me so much worry, you'll have to pay me back," she explained. "I want you to weed the flower bed in front of the house. If you get started right now, you should be finished in time for dinner."

Alan was distressed and, like most hyperactive children, did not hide his distress well. Grumbling and sulking, he set about weeding the flower bed. For fifteen minutes he weeded in a halfhearted fashion, at best. His pace quickened considerably, however, after his mother appeared on the front porch and informed him pleasantly that she hoped he would finish in an hour so he wouldn't miss dinner. An hour later, the job completed to his mother's satisfaction, Alan sat down to dinner with his family.

How to Use Negative Consequences. If negative consequences don't seem to have much of an effect on your child's behavior, part of the problem may lie with the way you have been using them.

After a trying day, you have just collapsed on the couch to read the paper. Dinner's over, the dishes have been washed and put away, and you have ten minutes all to yourself. The kids are playing on the floor, Peter with his big trucks, Sarah with building blocks.

Out of the corner of your eye, you notice that Peter is moving his trucks with increasing force, occasionally bumping them into the walls and furniture. "Oh, no," you think, "no more trouble. I'm just too tired to handle it. Maybe if I just ignore it, he'll stop."

But Peter, being Peter, doesn't stop—he never does. With your last ounce of patience you say, "Peter, please stop being so rough with your trucks." No reply. The bumps become thumps. "Peter!" you warn in a louder tone. Still no reply. The thumps become crashes.

Then the inevitable happens: Peter crashes a truck into his sister's block structure, sending blocks tumbling everywhere. His sister shrieks in protest. You explode. "Dammit!" you yell, leaping up from the couch. "Can't you ever listen to me? I've had it with you." Grabbing him roughly by the arm, you jerk him toward the stairs. "Get up those stairs and get ready for bed. I don't even want to have to look at you any more today."

Peter stomps up the steps and into his room, slamming the door. You sink into a chair, shaken and upset. "It never ends," you think. "It just never, never ends."

This little scenario illustrates several mistakes parents make in using negative consequences.

• *Ignoring misbehavior usually doesn't work.* Mental health professionals often advise parents to ignore problem behavior on the assumption that the behavior will weaken and die out if it is not reinforced with attention. Most parents, however, find that this is difficult to do and, with hyperactive children, usually ineffective. Like Peter, the child in the example, hyperactive children have problems putting the brakes on their own behavior. Parents, then, have to do this for the hyperactive child by intervening actively when misbehavior occurs.

Of course, there are some exceptions. For example, one of the best tactics for handling tantrums, especially in public places, is to simply walk away from the child. For most other kinds of problem behavior, though, active intervention is better than trying to ignore something that probably won't go away by itself.

• *Don't nag.* Telling a child the same thing over and over is exasperating and inefficient. Children quickly learn to tune out parents who nag. When you want your child to stop what he is doing, don't give repeated warnings: tell him once, pleasantly but firmly, to stop. Tell him what the consequences will be if he doesn't stop, then be prepared to impose the consequences immediately.

• *Intervene early.* Don't wait until you are out of patience and your child is out of control before stepping in. The time to intervene is as early as possible. Although some parents object, "But I'd be on his back constantly if I stepped in for every little thing," intervening quickly to redirect the child greatly reduces the number of times you will actually have to impose negative consequences.

• *Suggest and reinforce appropriate alternatives.* Because hyperactive children find it so hard to inhibit their behavior, it is usually easier for them to stop doing something if they are redirected into another activity. For example, the parent in the example might have said, "Peter, no rough play in the living room. If you want to play with your trucks, please take them into your bedroom. If you stay in this room, you can watch television or you can color with your new crayons."

Such redirecting is much more successful if it is accompanied by actual physical guidance. Put your hand on the child's shoulder to gently propel him in the desired direction, for example, or help him pick up his toys to move them to another area.

• *Don't yell and scream.* You can't help your child control his behavior if you are not in control of your own. Ranting and raving will not get your point across more effectively—in fact, research conducted at the State University of New York at Stony Brook provides convincing evidence that exactly the opposite is true. Psychologists compared the effects of two kinds of negative consequences on the behavior of hyperactive children. The results were clear-cut: a so-called "prudent" approach (calm, concrete, and consistent) was much more effective than an approach the investigators termed "imprudent" (ignoring misbehavior too long, then responding inconsistently and in a loud, emotionally upset fashion). Under conditions of imprudent negative consequences, the children's behavior deteriorated so dramatically that, although this phase of the research was very brief, the investigators reported that ethical concerns prevented them from extending it.

POINT PROGRAMS AND TOKEN ECONOMIES

Many professionals who use behavior modification methods with children suggest the use of point programs and "token economy" systems in which the child earns points, chips or tokens of some kind to "purchase" privileges and access to things he enjoys. A particular advantage of point programs is that consequences, in the form of giving or taking away points, can be delivered on the spot, regardless of where or when the behavior occurs. An additional advantage is that, since a point cost can be negotiated for virtually any kind of reinforcer, the list of potential reinforcers is enormous and reinforcers can be varied with ease.

Point programs, however, are not for everyone because they require a considerable amount of time, organization, and follow-through on the part of the adults involved. In fact, token economies were originally developed for use with psychiatric patients in residential institutions. In these settings, patients' behavior can be monitored closely and their access to privileges and activities strictly controlled. In the home setting, of course, it is much more difficult to monitor a child's every move and restrict his access to snacks, television viewing, and the like. This is especially true in single-parent families and families in which both parents work outside the home.

For this reason, the average family should probably avoid setting up complicated point programs as a daily management technique. Instead, it would be better to reserve point programs for specific problem behavior which seems to need special attention.

Jeremy desperately wanted a very expensive skateboard. His parents, equally desperate in their desire to see him succeed academically, negotiated a point program based on completing homework assignments. Jeremy could earn two points each day if he brought home a sheet initialed by his teacher indicating that he had completed and handed in his homework from the previous day. If Jeremy earned ten points (or the total possible number of points during weeks in which there were fewer than five school days), he could "rent" the skateboard for the following week. Otherwise, the skateboard would be locked in the closet for the week.

The program worked to everyone's satisfaction. During the entire school year, there were only two occasions when Jeremy failed to earn enough points to rent his beloved skateboard. His parents were pleased that Jeremy's grades improved, and Jeremy himself seemed proud of his good report cards.

In school, of course, the situation is quite different from that in the average home. Point programs and token economies are particularly appropriate for use in the school setting because:

• Daily routines and schedules are clearly established.
• The child is under adult supervision most of the day.
• Access to reinforcers such as recess and free time can be strictly controlled.

In fact, token economies and point programs are widely used in special classrooms in public schools across the United States. An excellent example is the token economy used in the classroom for hyperactive children at the National Institute of Mental Health in Bethesda, Maryland. This program, developed by classroom teacher Christine Leibner, is described in detail in Appendix A.

6

How Can the Family Help?

Daily Life with the Hyperactive Child

THE PROBLEMS PARENTS FACE

Like many parents, you've probably read at least a few books on child rearing, searching for answers. And, like many parents, you've probably been confused by the fact that no two "experts" seem to agree on much of anything. Conflicting advice and theories aside, however, there is one point on which the experts would certainly agree: parenting is a tough profession!

Only on television sitcoms are the children always perfectly behaved, the parents always cheery, warm, and perfectly understanding. In real life, *all* children occasionally act in ways that can drive a parent to despair. And *all* parents at times feel harassed, angry, resentful, anxious, disappointed, confused, and helpless.

How much more difficult, then, to be the parent of a hyperactive child, with his special needs and his exasperating behavior. Anyone who has ever lived with a hyperactive child knows that children with ADHD are often difficult, demanding, and exhausting. Their tendency to be forgetful, absentminded, and messy poses particular problems in a busy, active family in which both parents work and daily schedules are planned with no time to spare. Many hyperactive children are argumentative and exceptionally skilled in the art of debating ridiculous points, so a simple request to take out the trash or feed the dog can lead to a wrangle that only the Supreme Court could settle. Often these children have so little tolerance for frustration that any disappointment or difficulty, no matter how minor, can result in a blowup of major proportions.

But while children with ADHD can certainly be maddening, they can also be heartbreaking. To hear a child say, "I can't do anything. I'm so stupid. I wish I was dead!" or to try to comfort a child who sobs, "Nobody likes me. They call me 'retard' and 'spaz' " is a deeply painful experience for a parent.

Then, too, there are the problems parents face when their hyperactive child's behavior brings him into constant conflict with people outside of the immediate family. There is anger, shame, and embarrassment when:

• He is expelled from a preschool gymnastics class because he is unmanageable.

• Other shoppers aim disapproving looks at you because he is racing through the aisles or throwing a tantrum in the checkout line.

• Other parents in the neighborhood don't want their children to play with him.

• Even his grandparents won't take him for the day because he is so difficult, although they often take their other grandchildren for days at a time.

There is also confusion and bewilderment.

"His pediatrician told me it was just the 'terrible twos' and that he would outgrow it. My mother-in-law thinks we spoil him and that all he needs is a good spanking. But *my* mother says we're too hard on him; she says he's just all boy. His teachers complain that he's simply lazy, but the school counselor says the problem is a poor self-concept. A psychologist told us that we needed family therapy. My neighbor is sure it's food allergies: her nephew was the same way until they put him on a special diet."

And then there are the nagging fears. What will happen to him in the future? What will his life be like? He's failing fifth grade: how will he ever get into college? How will he support himself? What's going to become of him?

Because it is widely believed that the infant is like a slab of clay that is molded and shaped by the way in which he is raised, parents of hyperactive children often cannot help but feel an overwhelming sense of guilt and failure. "It's my fault somehow," you may have thought many times. "How did I go wrong?" Unfortunately, these feelings may be fed by friends, relatives, neighbors, teachers—even by the mental health professionals to whom you turn for help. Dr. Eugene Arnold, a child psychiatrist with great compassion for beleaguered parents, describes the predicament faced by many parents of hyperactive children: "Often the parents are presented with a "Catch-22" dilemma. If they assume [that their child is basically normal], they are forced to conclude—with the encouragement of the community—that they are miserable failures as parents. If they recognize the child's handicap and act logically on it, they may be labeled overprotective or overcontrolling. If they wear out, or if the child breaks away from their control, they may be labeled overpermissive."[27]

Parents may also feel guilty about their feelings of resentment, anger—even hatred, at times—toward the hyperactive child himself. Some parents are plagued by impulses to injure their hyperactive child. Some, of course, actually act on these impulses: among physically abused children, a disproportionate number suffer from ADHD. Other parents, fortunately, can recognize and control their angry impulses. For example, I know several parents of hyperactive children who have a no-spanking policy because, they explain, "If I were to hit him, I'm afraid I would kill him!"

Like a pebble tossed into a pond, the hyperactive child's problems cause ripples that often extend far beyond the child himself. Sometimes the frustration and resentment parents feel toward their hyperactive child is directed not toward the child himself but toward others. Outside the family, teachers are among the most common targets for this misplaced anger. Within the family, the other children may become scapegoats for the negative feelings their parents have toward the hyperactive child. Parents may accuse them of lack of concern for their hyperactive sibling, complain that they are selfish and uncaring, and demand the impossible in terms of patience and understanding.

One of the most tragic forms of misdirected hostility occurs when parents, in their confusion and frustration, blame each other for the problem. While one parent may complain, "You're too lenient with him; you don't discipline him enough," the other may counter with "You're too harsh with him. You're always yelling at him and picking on him." These problems can be amplified if the child behaves better for one parent than for the other. In these cases, it is usually the father who elicits better behavior: although there are certainly exceptions, hyperactive children tend to be somewhat more cooperative and less unruly with male adults. The reason for this is unclear, but Dr. Russell Barkley speculates that the father's physical size and strength may intimidate the child. He also points out that fathers may administer discipline more swiftly and intensely than mothers, many of whom try to reason with the child about his behavior.

Whatever the reason, this can be quite demoralizing to the frustrated mother of a hyperactive youngster, especially if her husband accuses her of incompetence as a disciplinarian. The mother who has spent a long, trying day coping with the behavior of an overactive, uncooperative child is not in the mood to hear, "I don't have any problems with him. Why can't you make him behave? You must be doing something wrong."

In other ways, too, the burden of raising a hyperactive child can strain a marriage, sometimes to the breaking point. Many parents find that the child's behavior makes it hard to obtain a baby-sitter, so they are unable to enjoy time alone or together as a couple. Mothers, especially, may be so worn out after a day of chasing after the child that they have little energy left over for their husbands. Sex, intimacy, closeness—all go by the board. When all leisure time must be spent in the presence of a difficult child, it is easy for parents to feel trapped and resentful. Patience wears thin, tempers fray, and arguments erupt, further eroding the marital relationship.

The "ripple effect" surrounding the hyperactive child can extend beyond the immediate family and affect relationships with the extended family as well, particularly if these relationships are already somewhat shaky. Some parents of hyperactive children learn to dread large family gatherings, knowing that the child will be compared unfavorably with his many cousins. They know, too, that they will have to listen to critical comments and unwanted advice. There is the no-nonsense grandfather who insists, "What that boy needs is to have his bottom fanned!" There may also be a doting grandmother who points out, "He's such an angel with me. I think you're too hard on him." And then there is the cousin who took a psychology course in college and is convinced that your child is schizophrenic. All of these well-intentioned people only add to parents' guilt and confusion.

Even if your child has been correctly diagnosed as having ADHD and is taking medication to help improve his behavior, there may be problems with the extended family. Some grandparents cannot acknowledge that there is anything wrong with their grandchild and object vigorously both to the diagnosis and to the idea that the child is being "drugged."

COPING WITH THE PROBLEMS

MANAGING YOUR OWN EMOTIONS

If your relationship with your hyperactive child is somewhat the worse for wear and tear, what steps can you take to change things? A good place to start is with your own emotional responses. Are you often angry with the child? Do you blow up when he misbehaves? Seethe with resentment because he causes so many problems?

While these feelings are understandable, you probably recognize that they contribute nothing positive to your relationship with your child. In fact, they interfere with your ability to manage your child's behavior: you can't deal effectively with an upset, irrational child if you become angry and upset yourself. But how can you rid yourself of this excess emotional baggage? How can you stay calm in spite of your child's trying behavior?

First, you must recognize that your child doesn't make you angry: you make yourself angry. In other words, you create your own anger by adopting a certain attitude about your child's behavior. If, for example, you tell yourself, "How awful that he's behaving this way. It's horrible. I can't stand it!" then the resulting emotion is bound to be anger. On the other hand, if you merely tell yourself, "This is an unfortunate nuisance" or "This is inconvenient," you avoid working yourself into a rage.

Unfortunately, most of us are in the habit of telling ourselves some unhelpful things about events that happen to us, and, as a consequence, we often add emotional upset to a situation that is already sufficiently unpleasant. We tell ourselves, for example:

"It's not fair!" (Of course it isn't. Did you get a guarantee that life would be fair?)

"He *shouldn't* behave that way." (Whether or not he should is irrelevant: he *is* behaving "that way.")

"I can't stand it!" (Yes, you can. It's unpleasant but it's not the end of the world.)

"How terrible that he's like this in public. Everyone will think I'm a bad mother—and that would be dreadful!" (Is the approval of others a dire necessity? Is it really a tragedy if total strangers think you are less than perfect?)

Changing deeply entrenched ways of thinking about your life situation can be extremely difficult. But you *can* change the way you respond to your child, and, in doing so, you can spare yourself a lot of unnecessary emotional turmoil. If you are persistent in your efforts, you can avoid that vicious cycle of anger and hostility which is so destructive to your relationship with your child and which leaves you feeling so ashamed and guilty.

A strategy that may help in your efforts is offered by Dr. John Taylor, who suggests, "Remind yourself that everyone has problems in life. There is no particular injustice in the fact that you are facing the problem of hyperactivity. Don't stop to ask fruitless questions about the justice of it all. The answer to 'How could this happen to me?' is, 'Very easily, because it *is* happening.'"[28]

It helps, too, to remind yourself that your child is not out to get you. He is not misbehaving deliberately just to make your life miserable. Like the rest of us, children want acceptance and approval. When a child fails in these areas, I believe that it is because he *can't* do what is expected of him, not that he *won't*. This assumption can have a powerful effect on how you approach problem behavior. If you believe that your child is willfully misbehaving, you are likely to feel frustrated and angry and become locked into no-win power struggles. On the other hand, if you assume that your child *cannot* comply with your demands, you will look for ways to guide and assist him so that he can succeed.

Finally, if you are often angry with your hyperactive child, it may help to try to identify the real source of the anger and upset. Anger is really a "secondary" emotion. If you examine your anger, you may find that it masks other emotions, such as:

• *Fear.* Fear and anger are closely related emotions, and the two often become confused. In very frightening situations, it is not uncommon for people to react with anger or rage as well as—or even instead of—fear. In a crisis, this substitution of anger for fear may have survival value because fear can paralyze us, while anger may galvanize us into necessary action:

In the yard of a small house in Arizona, a toddler played contentedly in the late spring sunshine. His parents, working nearby, were unaware of the rattlesnake only inches from their son until the baby's laughter caused them to look up. The baby's mother stood frozen with fear, unable to move or even scream but her husband sprang into action. As he raced forward, he grabbed a large flowerpot and hurled it at the snake, stunning it. Cursing violently, he stomped on the snake, grinding it beneath his heavy boots. Only long after the snake was dead did he cease stamping and swearing, and only then did he realize that he was trembling from head to foot.

But, while anger can be lifesaving in an emergency, it is out of place and actually counterproductive in most situations in daily life. Even so, many people continue to confuse fear and anger. They cannot admit to themselves or others that they are afraid. They deal with feelings of fear by expressing their fear as anger. They find it less frightening to lash out in anger than to acknowledge and confront their fear.

It's quite true that the hyperactive child who is impulsive and heedless of danger gives his parents many legitimate reasons to worry. But many of a parent's anger-arousing fears are not based on concern for the child's physical safety. You know, for example, that your child won't die from a bad report card—but you worry that, without an education, he will spend his life doing menial labor. You know that he won't catch the plague if he is careless with his personal hygiene— but you fear that in later years others will shun him. You know that he won't be hanged for throwing rocks at the neighbor's garage—but you cringe when you picture him behind bars as an adult.

These half-acknowledged fears may be at the root of much of your anger and impatience with your hyperactive child. But think about it: instead of hiding them beneath a smoke screen of anger, wouldn't it be better to bring these feelings out in the open? Fears and worries often shrink to manageable proportions when you face them squarely. If you find that concern for your child's future causes you to overreact to situations in the present, make a conscious effort to stay in the here and now. Deal only with the problem at hand, not the one you anticipate twenty years from now.

• *Disappointment.* Anger can also be a response to dashed hopes and frustrated expectations. It is disappointing when your child's behavior disrupts a special occasion. It hurts when he responds to your efforts to help him by shouting, "Leave me alone!" It is frustrating when he fails again and again to meet your expectations.

Yet covering the hurt and disappointment with anger won't make these feelings go away. Like fear, these feelings are easier to deal with when they are acknowledged and accepted as normal. You may find it helpful to talk about these feelings with your spouse or an understanding friend.

It helps, too, to prevent constant disappointment by frequently checking your expectations of the child against the reality of his abilities. It's hard to remember to do this because the hyperactive child looks so normal that we tend to forget his limitations and assume that he is capable of meeting "normal" expectations. A reminder: when you find yourself constantly frustrated and disappointed with your child, let this be a red flag that you may be overestimating his abilities and setting yourself up for disappointment.

• *Depression.* Anger and irritability are sometimes symptoms of depression. We all feel depressed at times, especially after a bad day—and parents of hyperactive children have more than their share of bad days. The syndrome of clinical depression is more than just a passing low mood, however: it is an illness that has other symptoms associated with it. Sleep disturbances, including difficulty falling asleep, poor or restless sleep, and early morning awakening, are very common in depressed people. Stomach ailments are common, as is loss of appetite and weight. Menstrual changes in women and lowered sex drive are also encountered. Loss of interest or pleasure in usual activities and withdrawal from friends and family are usually observed, as well as feelings of fatigue and decreased energy. Even small tasks may be difficult for the depressed person to accomplish. A major symptom of depression is a pessimistic view of the future and a tendency to exaggerate current difficulties. Other symptoms include difficulty concentrating, brooding, anxiety, and excessive preoccupation with physical health.

If you would like more information about depression and the treatment methods available, the National Institute of Mental Health publishes a very informative booklet entitled "Depression: What We Know." Single copies of this booklet can be obtained at no charge by writing to:

Public Inquiries Branch
Room 15C-05
National Institute of Mental Health
5600 Fishers Lane
Rockville, MD 20857

IMPROVING RELATIONSHIPS WITH OTHERS IN THE FAMILY

Your Relationship with Your Marriage Partner. Because the stresses of raising a hyperactive child can put so much pressure on a marriage, your relationship with your spouse may need special attention. Over the years, I've learned to expect blank stares and long silences when I ask the parents of a hyperactive youngster, "How long has it been since you've spent a weekend—or even an evening—without the kids?" Even when parents do spend time alone together, too often this precious time is spent discussing the hyperactive child and his problems. If your preoccupation with your child's problems spills over into your time together as a couple, try planning activities that force your attention elsewhere. Do something active: it's hard to worry about problems at home when you're piloting a raft through white water. Go ice skating or bowling or canoeing. Go to a play or a movie. Then go out for a drink or a snack afterwards and talk about the show. Spend an evening with friends who have no children: if you are tempted to discuss your child's difficulties at length, the glazed looks will force a quick change in conversational topics.

What about arguments that center on how to handle the child? Sometimes disagreements occur because parents have different expectations of the child. A father might be inclined to view his son's behavior as "just being a boy," especially if he himself was a hyperactive youngster. Or it may be that the father simply isn't around the child as much as his wife is or, as previously noted, the child may be somewhat better behaved when Dad is around. In some families, the opposite is true: instead of urging her husband to take a firmer stand with the child, the mother finds herself serving as a referee between the child and a father she considers too harsh and unreasonable.

In many cases, negotiation and compromise are possible. But bear in mind that you probably won't be able to reach an agreement if you try to blame, shame, or bludgeon your partner into doing things your way. An angry, accusatory tone will just put your partner on the defensive, and when people feel defensive, they are likely to counterattack rather than cooperate. A person who feels defensive is not likely to listen with an open mind, nor is he likely to consider changing his attitudes or his behavior. Instead, he is apt to cling even more tenaciously to his present beliefs and behaviors. How can you talk about the problem without putting your partner on the defensive?

• *Describe the problem without blaming or judging your partner.* Talk about what you have *observed* instead of labeling your partner or second-guessing his motives. Avoid pejorative labels like "selfish," "childish," and "irresponsible."

POOR: "If you weren't so wrapped up in your job, you'd spend more time with your son."
BETTER: "You know, in the past couple of months, you and Johnny haven't spent much time together. Is something wrong?"

POOR: "Why do you have to be such a perfectionist? You're on her case all day long—nag, nag, nag."
BETTER: "I've noticed that you and Sarah seem to be having a lot of disagreements lately. I'm concerned because neither of you seems very happy."

• *Use a problem-solving approach.* Emphasize sharing information and ideas instead of just giving instructions and advice. If your attitude smacks of "I-know-best-so-I'll-tell-you-what-to-do," you are almost certain to encounter resistance. On the other hand, if you approach the situation as a problem the two of you can work on together, you're more likely to gain your partner's cooperation.

INSTEAD OF:	SAY:
I think you should . . .	Let's discuss how we might . . .
You really ought to . . .	What do you think about . . .

I want you to . . .   I'd like to explore some ways to . . .
Why don't you . . .   I'd like to hear your ideas about . . .

• *Focus on feelings.* How does your partner feel when your child misbehaves? Beneath all the shouts and the anger, is there fear for the child's future? Does the child's behavior threaten your husband's image of himself as a strong, competent male (*"My* father would never have stood for that, I can tell you!")? Or perhaps it's your wife whose self-esteem is in jeopardy ("If I were a better mother, he wouldn't behave like that"). Bringing these feelings into the open is an important first step in working on the problem.

Of course, you can't understand how your partner feels unless you make an honest effort to see things from his or her point of view. This is difficult because we tend to think of our own point of view as the only reasonable or right way to see things. It's hard to remember that others have as much right to their feelings and perceptions as we do. It will require real effort on your part to put aside your own view and to try to see things through your partner's eyes. It helps to ask yourself, "How does this situation look to my partner? How am I coming across to my partner right now? What do I know about my partner's values, hopes, fears, and worries that would help me understand his or her feelings?"

You can also encourage discussion of feelings by talking about your own feelings: "When Timmy acts up in public, I get embarrassed. I worry about what other people must think. It's really hard for me to stay calm and just do the best I can." Or, "Telephone calls from Sandy's teacher are tough for me to handle. I get angry and upset but I guess it's because I'm worried that she's never going to make it through school."

Helping Brothers and Sisters Cope. Brothers and sisters of hyperactive children often complain, "You let him get away with stuff I'd never get away with. How come he never has to do anything around here?" Jealousy and competition exist in all families, and "It's not fair!" is one of the most common cries in any household where there are children. The problem is apt to be especially pronounced in families with a hyperactive child because there may well be obvious inequities. You probably *do* have to devote more of your time and attention to his needs than to the needs of the others. It's likely that you *don't* expect as much of the hyperactive child as you do of the others. How can you handle the inevitable complaints from the other children in the family?

Although it's obviously impossible to keep everything in the family scrupulously even and "fair," some parents fall into this trap—usually with very unhappy results. I have even known parents who requested that I schedule appointments for their other children because the children complained, "It's not fair: he gets to go there and play with all those neat toys in Dr. Ingersoll's office and I don't!"

As Louise Bates Ames, cofounder of the Gesell Institute, points out, "Any parent who allows himself to play the fairness game has had it, right from the start." Life itself, she notes, is not fair, so why teach children that it is or that it should be? Don't play the game. Refuse to be drawn into lengthy debates about whether or not something is "fair." A good response to wails of "It's not fair!" is "It probably isn't, but I'm doing the best I can so you'll just have to make do with that."

It is also common for brothers and sisters of hyperactive youngsters to complain that the hyperactive child intrudes on their privacy, takes their belongings, and even that he physically attacks and hurts them. All too often, brothers and sisters attempt to settle the score with their fists. As the authority figures in the family, parents do have an obligation to protect the property rights and physical security of all members of the family. If locks are needed to insure privacy and protect property, use them. If the hyperactive child is too rough with his siblings, closer supervision is necessary, even if this means that you must hire someone to supervise the children while you attend to household chores. Otherwise, you might have to insist that the children play in separate rooms when you are not able to provide direct supervision.

In other families, parents may refuse to play referee and may opt to let the children settle their own differences. As the parents of a hyperactive child, however, you may not be able to afford this luxury. Household rules should be clear: no roughhousing (it inevitably leads to bruises and tears); no name calling; no hitting, pinching, poking, kicking, or shoving. Enforce these rules swiftly and firmly. Don't ask who started it: "He hit me first" does *not* excuse hitting back.

What about the child who is embarrassed by his hyperactive brother or sister? Children are often blunt to the point of cruelty. "How come your brother is so weird?" they ask. "What's wrong with your sister? Is she retarded or something?" These questions can be particularly humiliating to a teenager because adolescents are often painfully self-conscious and dread being viewed as different in any way from their peers. Your job as a parent is to help the other children in the family understand that they are not responsible for the hyperactive child's actions and that, if others judge them on the basis of the hyperactive child's behavior, their opinions are not worth caring about. Along these lines, Dr. John Taylor offers good advice: "The other children must learn to stand aside psychologically so that they are not in the middle between your [hyperactive] child and others who are upset by [the hyperactive child's] behavior. Suggest to the other children that when someone makes comments to them about your [hyperactive] child, they should ask the other person to make those comments directly to him. Other children need feel no obligation to explain, excuse, justify, apologize for, or be embarrassed by your [hyperactive] child's behavior; the aftereffects of his behavior are his own responsibility."[29]

Of course, you can help your children with these feelings only to the extent that you have come to grips with your own feelings of embarrassment. If you still want to sink into the ground when your hyperactive child acts up in a public place

—if you still tell yourself "How awful that these total strangers think I'm a bad parent"—you won't come across to your children as very convincing.

In general, how much cooperation and understanding can you reasonably expect from the other children in the family? This depends to a great extent on the age, sex, and personality of each of the children. There is usually more rivalry and competition between siblings who are close in age than when several years' difference in age exists. Although there are exceptions, it is probably not realistic to expect an eight-year-old to be tolerant when his six-year-old brother grabs a toy away from him or destroys his art project. Nor will reasoning be of much avail. The explanation "He can't help it" doesn't make much sense to other children. Children firmly believe that all acts are intentional: to a young child, the explanation "He didn't do it on purpose; it was an accident" is incomprehensible. The bottom line is "He did it—period."

Although appeals to reason are not likely to get you very far, reinforcing cooperative behavior just might. Begin by enlisting the cooperation of the other children in the family. Explain to them that the hyperactive child has trouble learning to behave properly and that, when someone has trouble learning how to do something, teaching is a more sensible approach than punishing or yelling or hitting. Point out that people learn better and faster when others praise what they do right. You might ask, for example, "How do you feel when you've worked hard on something and I give you a big hug and say 'I'm really proud of you'?"

Discuss the areas in which the hyperactive child needs to improve and come up with a list of specific behaviors to reinforce. For instance, if the hyperactive child has difficulty playing cooperatively, a list of desirable behavior might include sharing toys, taking turns, following the rules, and not getting mad when someone else wins.

Encourage siblings to watch the hyperactive child closely to "catch him doing something good" and instruct them to praise good behavior quickly and frequently. Rehearse things to say and do to reinforce good behavior. Some examples include:

"I like it when you play by the rules."

"Thank you for sharing that with me. You can play with my fire truck if you want to."

"It's fun to play with you when you let me have a turn, too."

"That was nice of you to let me go first."

Of course, you will want to give your "agents" lots of reinforcement for being such good teachers. You can also encourage "reverse tattling": when a sibling spots the hyperactive child engaged in some desirable activity, in addition to praising the hyperactive child directly, the sibling should also report the good behavior to you immediately. This gives you the opportunity to reinforce both the hyperactive child and your "agent"—a double whammy!

Don't be afraid to expand into areas of behavior that don't directly involve the other children, once they have learned the knack of reinforcing good behavior. If, for example, personal hygiene is a problem for the hyperactive child, brothers and sisters can provide positive feedback when the hyperactive child's appearance is acceptable. For instance:

"Benjie, you look nice in those clean clothes."

"Katie, your hair looks so pretty. Did you just wash it?"

This approach—using brothers and sisters as reinforcing agents—may sound like pie in the sky to you at first, especially if open warfare currently exists among the children in your family. However, it is fairly simple: just remember to reinforce, reinforce, reinforce. Invest a little time and effort, and you may be astonished at the results you achieve.

HOW DO OTHER PARENTS COPE?

No matter how much experience a professional has had working with hyperactive children, he or she lacks the experience of actually living with a hyperactive child. It is parents, not professionals, who are on the front lines. Professionals, like football coaches, can provide support, advice, and guidance, but it is parents who must "carry the ball."

As parents cope with the ups and downs in the daily life of a hyperactive child, they accumulate a fund of practical knowledge and hands-on expertise. To tap this wealth of experience, we asked parents of hyperactive children to respond to a questionnaire. What, we asked them, have you found useful in dealing with your hyperactive child? What advice or tips would you give other parents of hyperactive children? Here are the replies.

Help the child organize himself.

• Keep your child's room furnished simply: the more furniture, toys, and books, the harder it is to clean and to find things he needs.

• Homework sheets have been very helpful for us. Russ writes down each assignment and has his teacher initial it. After his dad goes over each assignment, he initials it and the homework sheet goes back to school.

• Our child needs everything spelled out for him. He has a chart on his bedroom door with his chores listed. He also has a list of school-related tasks that must be done each night, such as make school lunch, put schoolbag by front door, lay out clothes for morning, and so on. We have to check on him, but just having the routine seems to help a lot.

Recognize the child's limits.

• Don't compare your child with other children. Try to remember that many of his actions are not done on purpose.

Although he must be disciplined, he shouldn't be made to feel guilty for things beyond his control.

• Try to think ahead in situations in which your child might have problems. Don't put your child in impossible situations. If Grandma has dozens of knickknacks all over the house and won't put them out of reach when you visit, *don't visit.* In any situation, watch for signs that your child is becoming over-stimulated and be prepared to remove him before the trouble starts.

• Make your expectations fit the child, not the other way around. Forget about what your child "should" be able to do and stick with the reality of what he actually is able to do. For example, even if other children his age can dress themselves in the morning, your child may not be able to do this without your help. Either realize this and adjust your morning schedule so you can help him or be prepared for a big scene every day—the choice is yours.

Boost your child's self-esteem.

• My son seems to need constant encouragement and assurance that he's okay. I have to remember to compliment him whenever possible. When there are little disasters all around you, it's hard to pull out something positive, but I'm really working on this in our relationship.

• Foster any activity in which your child excels, such as sports, music, art, or drama. Get the child involved in youth activities at your church or synagogue, where supportive people will express appreciation for the child's contributions.

• Adopt a family pet. Pets don't criticize children for their poor behavior, but they do offer unconditional love—and petting an animal is good for your blood pressure.

Work cooperatively with teachers and school counselors.

• It's not always easy to work with the school system: since they can't physically see the problem, they tend to treat it as if it didn't exist. You have to do your best to explain the problem to your child's teacher all over again every year. It really helps if your pediatrician or your child's therapist is willing to work with the school.

• Parents need to know the laws regarding public education. Our child is finally receiving the special services he needs in school, but it took a lot of pushing on our part.

• Joel's teacher sends a behavior checklist home with him every day. This helps us keep track of how he's doing. If there's a problem, we can take steps to correct it immediately. This is also much better than telephone calls from the teacher because you know about his good behavior, not just the bad.

• We have found that paying attention to the child's schedule is important. Try to arrange for the child to take the most demanding classes at the time of day when medication is most effective.

Simplify, set priorities, and keep things in perspective.

• Learn how to set priorities; decide what's important and what doesn't really matter. This is especially important for high-achieving families who despair that their hyperactive child is falling behind in the competition to win admission to a prestigious college.

• Jeanette definitely has a mind of her own and can be unbelievably stubborn about what she wants to do. We used to fight about every little thing until my sister told me, "You can't win every battle, so pick the ones you can afford to lose and *let go.*" Now before I get into an argument with her, I ask myself, "Is this really important? Is this really worth a fight?" If it is important, we insist that she do as she's told. But on the little, picky things like what she's going to wear to school or whether she can wear nail polish, why invest the energy in a big fight?

• I think holidays can be difficult for hyperactive children because they get too wound up and out of control. Keep things simple and low-key around holidays, especially Christmas. If you wear yourself out with cooking, baking, decorating, and shopping, you won't have the patience to deal with your child.

Ask for help when you need it.

• Though the Ritalin helps, it is not a cure-all. If you need counseling, get it. Remember that you are parents who want the best for your child and there is no shame in asking for outside help. It doesn't mean that you have failed but rather that you love your child so dearly that you are willing to obtain the help of professionals who have training and experience that you don't have.

• Don't be afraid to switch doctors if yours doesn't seem to understand the problem. We went to two pediatricians, a child psychiatrist, and a child psychologist before we found someone who could really help. Things aren't perfect now, but they are much better.

• Our health plan has a support group for parents that meets for ten weeks. This was very worthwhile for us. Meeting other parents of hyperactive children helped us feel like we weren't the only ones in the world with the problem.

• Behavior modification has been a lifesaver for our family. This kind of professional help is a good investment for anyone who has a hyperactive child.

Take care of yourself.

• Ignore self-appointed experts. Avoid people who try to make you feel guilty for putting your child on medication.

• Forgive yourself when, because of fatigue or overwork, you lose your patience or allow yourself to become embroiled in a senseless quarrel with your child.

• Get a baby-sitter occasionally for a weekend away. It does wonders for your overall frame of mind.

7

Special Problems of the Hyperactive Child

WETTING AND SOILING

WETTING (ENURESIS)

Exact figures are not available but it is estimated that between one third and one half of hyperactive children continue to have problems with bladder control long past the age when most other children are dry through the day and night. Bed wetting, sometimes lasting well into the teen years, is especially common in hyperactive children. Daytime wetting is less common, especially in older children, but about one third of younger bed wetters also have bladder accidents during the day.

Parents often search for physical causes—and cures—for wetting, but in only a small percentage of cases is there an obvious medical reason for the problem, such as a urinary tract infection. However, many children who have a problem with wetting do have a smaller bladder capacity and have to urinate more frequently than children without such problems. (This may explain why some children who bed wet are wet again only an hour or two after being awakened to urinate.) It also appears that these children are less sensitive to signals from their bladder indicating a need to urinate.

Daytime Wetting. If your child wets during the day, it is important to identify the pattern of accidents before you begin to work on the problem. For at least two weeks, keep a record of all accidents, noting time of day and circumstances (playing outdoors, riding in the car, and so on).

Some hyperactive children may wet simply because they are reluctant to interrupt their play for something as mundane as going to the bathroom. If the record indicates that this might be the case with your child, a reward program paired with positive practice should be helpful. With this approach, the child earns a small reward in the evening if he has remained dry during the day. If he has an accident, however, he will have to "practice" as soon afterwards as possible. For example, if the accident occurred while he was playing in the yard, he should walk quickly from the yard to the bathroom, remove his pants, and go through the motions of urinating, then return to the yard to start over. Ten repetitions of this procedure should follow every accident.

If this method is not helpful, or if your child has accidents at times other than when he is "too busy" to go to the bathroom or seems to dribble urine during the day, he may have poor sphincter control. If he urinates frequently and in small amounts during the day, the problem may be small bladder capacity. The following program can be helpful with both problems, and can be used with both boys and girls:

• For three days, record the time of day and the amount each time the child urinates. (Have the child urinate into a clear plastic measuring cup marked in units of 1/2 ounce.) Record the largest amount of urine and use that as the "record" to be beaten on the fourth day.

• On the fourth day, explain the "holding-back game" to the child: tell him that each time he feels the urge to urinate, he should hold off as long as possible. This way, you explain, he will be training his bladder to hold more and the amount will be larger when he finally urinates. The point of the game is to beat his previous record each time he urinates. Use stickers, stars, or points to be traded in for treats to reward each success.

• Each time the child urinates, have him practice stopping and starting the stream of urine. Explain that this will help strengthen the muscle that controls urination.

• Encourage the child to drink more fluids during the day. Explain that this will help his bladder get bigger and stronger.

• Continue to record accidents and use the positive practice approach for each accident.

Continue the program until daytime wetting is no longer a problem. This usually happens by the time the child is consistently able to hold about 10–14 ounces per voiding.

Bed wetting. While daytime wetting can be a source of much shame and embarrassment to a child, the child who is a bed wetter also suffers considerable damage to his self-esteem, especially if he is ridiculed or harshly punished. For the hyperactive child who is in constant conflict with his environment and whose self-esteem is already low, bed wetting may seem like one more failure in a long series of failures. For his beleaguered parents, it's just one more frustration, one more indication that this child can't do anything right.

Kendrick was mortified when he learned that his little sister had told her friends that he wet his bed. It was tough enough to pretend that he didn't care about failing so many tests in school or that Mrs. August always yelled at him for daydreaming in class. It was especially hard to act "cool" when he was the last one chosen for recess kickball games and to ignore the snickers and taunts of "spaz" when he tripped or missed the ball.

But this—this was too much! He knew the other fifth-graders would be merciless when the word got around. Especially Brian Gavin. He'd get all the others to gang up—Kendrick shuddered when he imagined it.

"Maybe," he thought, "if I pray real hard I won't be wet when I wake up tomorrow." But he knew it wouldn't work. Nothing else had worked. Even his parents had finally given up and just tried to act like it didn't matter. It did, though: he could tell by the look on his mother's face each time she changed his wet sheets.

Before you begin any kind of treatment program to help your child learn nighttime dryness, have a heart-to-heart talk with your child about the problem. Assure him that bed wetting doesn't mean that he is bad or lazy or a baby. You might also tell him that he is not alone: in a class of thirty children, three or four are still bed wetting at five and six years of age; in the average fourth- or fifth-grade classroom, two children still have the problem.

It's also a good idea to keep careful records of bed wetting for at least two weeks—preferably even longer—before starting to work on the problem. Later, as the child sees concrete proof of his progress, it will help keep interest and motivation high.

Two of the most successful methods for treating bed wetting are the urine alarm and a procedure called "dry bed training." Based on the idea that the child needs to learn to recognize and respond to bladder signals, the *urine alarm**
consists of a moisture-sensitive pad on which the child sleeps. When the pad is moistened with a few drops of urine, it triggers an alarm. The alarm awakens the child (or the parent) and the child gets up and goes, or is taken, to the bathroom. Eventually, the child learns to respond to the cues of a full bladder without the assistance of the alarm.

* The urine alarm system is available from Montgomery Ward and Sears, Roebuck. Prices range from $30 to $50 for the equipment. Instructions are included.

Using the urine alarm, 80–90 percent of children achieve dryness after five to twelve weeks of treatment. Relapses do occur, but most children respond quickly when the alarm is reintroduced. "Overlearning" seems to enhance results and prevent relapses, so the more opportunities the child has to practice, the better. Opportunities to practice can be increased by increasing the child's fluid intake slightly in the early evening. Of course, a reward program will also help by keeping motivation high. In addition, some experts suggest that parents obtain guidance from a knowledgeable professional to assist with any problems that might arise.

Dry bed training is a multifaceted program aimed at increasing the child's bladder capacity as well as teaching him to respond to bladder signals. This method, which is too complex to be described in detail here,* involves several steps, including:

• Increasing daytime fluids to create a frequent desire to urinate
• Training in "holding back" during the day to increase bladder capacity and to teach sensitivity to bladder signals
• Hourly awakenings during the first night (intensive training), followed by progressively later awakenings on subsequent nights
• Use of a urine alarm (although the originators of dry bed training state that the use of a urine alarm is optional, results are apt to be much less satisfactory if the urine alarm is omitted)

Dry bed training appears to produce results more rapidly than the urine alarm alone, but some parents might find it too complicated. As with the urine alarm approach, the use of a reward system is strongly encouraged, and professional su-

---

* Detailed instructions for dry bed training are provided in an excellent book, *A Parent's Guide to Bedwetting Control: A Step-by-Step Method* (Nathan Azrin and Victoria Besalel, Pocket Books, 1981).

pervision can make the difference between success and failure for some families.

In addition to the behavioral programs, the antidepressant medication imipramine (Tofranil) is sometimes used to treat bed wetting. The dose range is usually 10–75 milligrams a day, although some children require as much as 125 milligrams a day. Some scientists believe that this drug works by correcting an imbalance of neurotransmitters in the brain, thereby correcting signals between the brain and the bladder.

In the majority of cases, there is an immediate reduction in the frequency of wetting, although only about one third achieve total dryness with medication. Some children who show an immediate positive response develop tolerance to the medication after two to six weeks, and frequency of wetting again increases.

Medication is *not* a cure for bed wetting: when medication is stopped, bed wetting occurs again almost immediately. However, medication can be useful on an occasional basis for events like sleepovers and camp or as a last resort for the child who has not been helped by other methods.

SOILING (ENCOPRESIS)

As the nurse ushered them into Dr. Benson's office, Mrs. Frey had to practically drag nine-year-old Timothy. "Tim, you don't look happy to be here today," Dr. Benson remarked. Tim looked at the doctor and shook his head. "Tell the doctor why you're here," his mother instructed. Tim hung his head and remained silent. "Tell her," his mother repeated. "You know why you're here." Tim only shook his head. Mrs. Frey made it clear to her son that he had stretched her patience to the limit. Through clenched teeth she insisted, "You *do* know why you're here. Now tell the doctor what you do." Tim kept his head down so they couldn't see the glisten of tears. In a small voice he admitted, "I poop in my pants."

Like wetting, soiling is not uncommon in hyperactive children. Also like wetting—and like ADHD itself—soiling is much more common in boys than in girls. Some children pass large, fully formed stools in their pants (or in other inappropriate places). Others pass only small amounts which may appear as stains or smears in their underwear. Most soiling takes place in the evening or after the child returns from school in the late afternoon. Stress and excitement seem to increase the likelihood that soiling will occur. The fact that the problem may wax and wane, with periods of soiling followed by long periods when no soiling occurs, is especially confusing and maddening to parents. "He's controlled it before, so he ought to be able to do it all the time," they conclude.

Most children who soil are chronically constipated. Prolonged stool retention or constipation results in a distended bowel (megacolon), impacted feces, and relaxed anal sphincter muscles. Fecal impaction may be so severe that there is a leakage of watery stool around the impaction, or block. This can appear to be diarrhea, and in fact a surprising number of these children are actually treated for diarrhea.

When the bowel is distended for long periods of time, the child seems to adapt to the sensation of fullness and is no longer sensitive to signals from the colon and rectum that indicate the need to have a bowel movement. This is why children who soil often insist "I didn't know I needed to go," which seems incomprehensible to their parents.

Many children who soil have a history of constipation beginning in infancy. As toddlers, many also seem afraid, or at least very reluctant, to use the toilet for bowel movements and may cry, cling, or throw tantrums if efforts are made to force them. Some refuse point-blank and may insist on being given a diaper in which to have a bowel movement. Since the history of these children usually reveals at least one episode of constipation or diarrhea resulting in a painful bowel movement, it is likely that these children have learned to fear the toilet in this manner.

For a problem which can cause so much frustration and unhappiness, soiling is actually surprisingly easy to treat in most cases. In several studies with large groups of children who soil, success rates in the neighborhood of 80–100 percent are reported. In my own practice, I've obtained excellent results with a simple approach which consists of a bowel cleanout, education, explanation, and retraining.

Step One: Explanation and Education. Like the child who wets, the child who soils usually believes that he is the only child in the world with the problem. He needs to be reassured that he is not alone, that many other children have similar difficulties. He also needs to know that he is not really at fault because the problem is due to a physical condition.

To explain the physical problems, you can use sketches to help the child understand how his intestines function. Draw a tube in cross section (a circle within a larger circle). Explain that the outer walls of the tube are muscle which moves waste along through the inner part of the tube. Tell the child that waste sometimes accumulates in the tube, perhaps because the child deliberately holds it in because he's too busy to go to the bathroom, or perhaps his diet doesn't contain the right things to keep the waste moving along the tube. Explain that when the waste gets stuck, it continues to accumulate, blocking the tube and causing it to bulge. This makes the muscles of the intestinal wall thin and weak, so they can't make the waste move along the tube. (Illustrate with a second sketch of a tube with a thinner outer wall.)

Tell your child that you are going to begin a program to help him build up the muscles in his intestinal walls and that, with consistent effort, he can learn to control his bowel movements as these muscles get stronger. Explain that the first step will be to get rid of the bulge which is currently blocking his intestines so that he can get off to a good start on his "muscle training program."

Step Two: Bowel Cleanout. Before beginning a retraining program, a medical evaluation is necessary to rule out the possibility that there is a medical problem involved and to begin a bowel cleanout regimen. To thoroughly empty the bowel of waste, a cleanout regimen of enemas, laxatives, and suppositories is used. It usually takes about two to three weeks of such a regimen to be certain that no waste is retained. (Some experts believe that an X ray is essential to be sure the bowel is empty because simply feeling the child's abdomen is not always an accurate way to detect retained feces.)

Step Three: Retraining. With children who are not afraid of the toilet, a retraining program involves the following:

• Select a set time each day—preferably 20–30 minutes after a meal—when your child will use the toilet.

• Decide what the daily consequences will be for performance and nonperformance. Elaborate rewards are not necessary: many families simply allow the child to earn privileges such as television time or access to other activities he enjoys. Other families like to use small sums of money to reward performance. I don't object to this, but I do insist that if money is used to reward success, a fine must be imposed for failure.

• Verify reports of success so your child is not tempted to "cheat." The mere sound of a toilet being flushed is not sufficient proof of performance.

• If your child does not have a bowel movement for two consecutive days, use a suppository so that the impaction process doesn't set in again.

• Be certain that your child's diet is high in bulk and fiber. Bran cereals, bran muffins, whole-grain breads, salads, raw vegetables, and cooked vegetables such as corn are all good sources. Popcorn is also an excellent source of bulk, and children are usually delighted to follow the recommendation to eat lots of popcorn on a regular basis.

This program usually produces excellent results within the first week or so. Although relapses may occur, they can usually be prevented through careful surveillance of diet and regular toilet habits.

Young children who are reluctant to use the toilet must be helped to overcome their fear before a retraining program can be started. For children who are very fearful and become greatly upset at the prospect of using the toilet, it's a good idea to seek professional help.

LYING AND STEALING

LYING

"I'm at the end of my rope with that kid. He knows I can't stand a liar. After all the times I've punished him for lying, you'd think he would finally learn. But, no! Even when you've got the proof right there in front of him, he'll still lie until he's blue in the face. I just don't understand it—*why* does he do it?"

Children lie for many reasons. The most common reasons for lying are to avoid punishment for misbehavior and to escape unpleasant tasks or chores.

Lying to Avoid Punishment. Almost all children will occasionally lie if they think that by lying they can avoid punishment and parental wrath. Experts agree that lying to avoid punishment is particularly likely to be a problem if a child is often subjected to expectations he cannot meet—a situation in which the hyperactive child frequently finds himself. The likelihood of self-protective lying is even greater if the child often receives harsh punishment for his misdeeds.

In an effort to teach the value of truthfulness, parents may tell their children that if they lie about a misdeed they will be punished twice, once for the misdeed and once for lying about it. When this tactic is used to elicit a confession, there are problems with it. Suppose your child then confesses his misdeed. If you impose any kind of punishment for the misdeed, you are in the awkward position of punishing your child for telling the truth. On the other hand, if you do not impose a punishment, you are in effect telling the child, "It's okay to break the rules as long as you tell the truth about it."

This tactic also tempts a child to play double-or-nothing. "If I admit I did it, I'll be punished for sure," your child may reason. "If I lie, I might be punished twice as hard, but I *might* get away with the lie and avoid any punishment altogether." For hyperactive children, especially, this gamble is often irresistible, even when the odds are clearly against them. In this area, as in others, hyperactive children are impulsive risk takers who seldom think through consequences before acting. This is particularly likely to be the case if there is any uncertainty about the consequences ("Maybe they won't find out").

Parents sometimes unintentionally tempt a child to lie by the way in which they confront him. To a child, the question "Did you break the lamp?" may sound like a genuine request for information, implying that you really have no idea who broke the lamp. In such a situation, the temptation to lie is almost too much for any child to resist.

In fact, we are *all* tempted to lie when asked to incriminate ourselves. Why, then, should we insist that a child testify against himself by demanding a confession from him? A more sensible approach would be to gather all the facts from other sources and make our decision based on this evidence.

But what if it is not clear whether your child is really at fault? Parents sometimes find themselves in the role of Grand Inquisitor when they suspect that the child has broken a rule but they lack full "proof" and do not want to punish him unfairly. Remember, decisions in this imperfect world cannot always be based on absolute certainty. If there is little evidence against your child, it is probably better to avoid the issue and simply forego discipline. However, if the evidence clearly points to your child as the culprit, impose a penalty for the rule violation. While your child may occasionally be punished unfairly, you can be sure that these occasions will be more than offset by the number of times he manages to avoid detection and gets off with no penalty for misdeeds he does commit.

If your child attempts to cover up a misdeed by lying, try not to be drawn into a game of "Courtroom" ("You know you did it." "No, honest, I didn't do it."). The wisest course is to impose a penalty for lying (work penalties are well suited to this purpose) and bring the discussion to an abrupt close. Later, when neither of you is upset, you and your child should discuss the importance of honesty among family members.

Lying to Avoid Unpleasant Tasks. Hyperactive children often lie to avoid unpleasant tasks and chores: "Yes, I took a shower (. . . I just didn't use any soap or water)"; "I already walked the dog (. . . last week)"; "I don't have any homework tonight (. . . it's not due until tomorrow)." Lies like these are particularly maddening to parents because they seem so senseless. "Why does he do it?" they ask. "He knows he can't get away with it. He knows he's going to be caught." And, indeed, he will be caught—just as soon as the dog wets on the rug an hour later or the teacher tells him to hand in his homework at 9:00 A.M. the next day.

Yet even though your child knows that unpleasant consequences are certain to follow, they may not seem very real to him since they are not immediate. To the child who lies to avoid doing his homework, for example, tomorrow is a long way away and—who knows—maybe the teacher will get sick or forget to ask for the homework or maybe the school will blow up or the world will end before tomorrow morning.

Parents are also bewildered by the lengths to which some hyperactive children will go to avoid tasks they dislike or consider particularly boring. The child who carefully wets his toothbrush and leaves the toothpaste tube sitting on the sink but doesn't actually brush his teeth is a good example. My own favorite is the youngster who was given the task of vacuuming the living room carpet while her parents went out for a few hours. Rather than fetch the vacuum from the hall closet, she worked her way across every inch of the large room, brushing up the nap of the carpet with her foot to give it a freshly vacuumed appearance. This method took at least ten times longer than it would have taken to simply vacuum the rug in conventional fashion. "But," she explained, "vacuuming is so *boring.*"

How can you cope with a child who lies to avoid tasks and chores? For the parent of a hyperactive child, forewarned is forearmed: it makes better sense to *assume* that the child will try to dodge dull tasks whenever he can. Therefore, close supervision rather than an honor system should be the rule for hyperactive children, at least in situations which parents know are particularly difficult for them. In other words:

DON'T ASK: "Did you clean your room?"
INSTEAD: Set a regularly scheduled time for daily room inspection. Post a list in the child's room of tasks to be accomplished by inspection time (e.g., bed made, clothes hanging on hooks or hangers in closet, etc.).

DON'T ASK: "Did you practice the piano today?"
INSTEAD: Have the child practice while you are at home, even if you are in another room. If you can't be there, have the child make a tape recording of her daily practice session. Then listen to the tape while you're cooking dinner or doing other household chores.

DON'T ASK: "Do you have homework tonight?"
INSTEAD: Ask the child's teacher to initial the child's assignment book daily (see Chapter 8). This way, you can be certain about what homework was assigned.

STEALING

It is probably safe to say that most young children experiment with stealing. Fortunately, most respond quite promptly to the time-honored practice of marching back to the scene of the crime, under parental escort, to return the stolen goods and apologize to the victim. By the age of six or so, most children have learned to curb their impulses and refrain from stealing.

Certainly not all hyperactive children steal. Many—probably the majority—respect the property rights of others. As a group, however, hyperactive children are more vulnerable to temptation than other children, for several reasons:

• *Poor impulse control.* Because impulse control is a particular problem for hyperactive youngsters, it is not surprising that some cannot seem to resist the temptation to help themselves to other people's property. (Note: stimulant medication is often useful in helping children who steal on impulse but is probably of little value for children who methodically work out plans in advance of stealing.)

• *Uncertain consequences.* If, as is usually the case, there are no witnesses on the scene, the potential consequences of stealing may seem remote or nonexistent: "How can I get caught if no one sees me?"

• *Little empathy for others.* Some hyperactive children are very self-centered. They find it difficult to put themselves in the place of a victim and to understand the suffering their behavior causes others.

• *Low self-esteem and poor social skills.* Children may steal to compensate for a lack of other positive things in their lives, such as affection, friendship, and respect for their abilities. Among hyperactive children who steal, a common pattern is to give away the stolen goods in an attempt to impress peers and buy friendship.

In our culture property rights are considered sacred, and violation of these rights is a serious offense. Parents are right to be worried about a child who habitually steals. At best, the child will earn a reputation in the community as a thief. At worst, he may end up in juvenile court. If your child continues to steal despite your best efforts to put an end to this behavior, it is time to take action immediately. What can you do?

• *Do not minimize the problem.* It may be hard for you to acknowledge that your child steals. Some parents cannot even bring themselves to use the word "steal," so they substitute words like "take" and "borrow." Stealing is stealing, whether it is a nickel from your purse or a $50.00 sweater from a department store.

• *Discuss the problem calmly.* Don't give a sermon. Don't yell, threaten, call the child names, and predict he'll end up in jail. *Talk* with the child. Tell him why you're so concerned—that other people won't like or trust him; that he'll lose friends; and that he will probably have to pay a high price in many ways for stealing. It may help, too, to point out how unfair it is to the victim and how bad people feel when they lose something of value to them.

• *Establish clear rules and penalties.* Do not allow the child to bring home "gifts" and things he has "found." Explain that all such items will be considered stolen and that a penalty will be imposed. Restitution should be part of any penalty for stealing, so work penalties are especially appropriate.

• *Provide supervision.* Child psychologist Gerald Patterson, at the University of Oregon, reports that many young thieves are "wanderers" who have a great deal of unsupervised time. Children who steal need close supervision, both to reduce the opportunities for stealing and to increase the likelihood of detection when they do steal. Thus, the child should expect regular room checks and even pocket searches until you are sure the problem has been corrected. This approach may seem distasteful to you, but it is not intended to be punitive. Like the methods recommended for other problems of the hyperactive child, support and prevention are preferable to punishment after the fact.

"NOBODY LIKES ME!"

In her own words, twelve-year-old Nancy was a "social reject." Even in preschool, her teachers noticed that she preferred to play by herself instead of joining the other children in art projects, circle time, and dramatic play. In elementary school, her disheveled appearance and messy desk made her the target of nasty comments and unflattering nicknames like "Nancy the Nerd." Sometimes, too, she was teased about the "babyish" toys she brought to school, about her learning problems, and about her poor skills at kickball, dodgeball, and other playground games.

Although there were several children Nancy's age in the neighborhood, they seldom included Nancy in their games and activities. If she played with anyone, it was usually younger children, but most of her time was spent at home in front of the television. When the girl next door had a birthday party, she invited Nancy but made it clear that the invitation was issued only because her parents insisted. Of course, Nancy had a miserable time at the party and returned home in tears.

Nancy's parents, concerned about their daughter's social isolation, encouraged her to join the church youth group and the Girl Scouts. Nancy flatly refused. She also rejected their repeated suggestions to invite classmates home, stating, "They hate me and I hate them."

Not all hyperactive children have problems like Nancy's. The hyperactive child with a sunny, outgoing disposition, for example, may have no trouble finding friends to play with, even if he is loud and boisterous. Similarly, the athletically skilled hyperactive child is often respected by his peers, who may accept his bossiness as leadership. Occasionally, fate intervenes and the hyperactive child "gets lucky."

No one in the neighborhood had the energy to keep up with Michael—no one, that is, until Edward moved in down the street. Like Michael, Edward's supply of energy was inexhaustible. After a morning spent racing through the neighborhood on bikes and an afternoon at the pool, Edward was still ready for a wild game of badminton in Michael's yard after supper. Only four months apart in age, the boys quickly became inseparable. In addition to boundless energy, the boys also had in common the hot temper which often characterizes hyperactive children, so loud arguments frequently punctuated their play. Neither seemed to hold a grudge, however, so the squabbles blew over as quickly as they began. Most often they were a team, united against Michael's older brother and his friends in water fights or plotting diabolical new ways to torment Edward's older sister.

Unlike Michael, most hyperactive children do not have the good fortune of finding a boon companion, and the same qualities that bring them into conflict with adults cause them to have problems in their relationships with other children. Home life in families with a hyperactive child may be marred by sibling battles that are far more frequent and intense than in other families. Brothers and sisters often complain bitterly about the hyperactive child—that he spoils holidays and family outings with his wild, unpredictable behavior, that he helps himself to their belongings, and that his antics embarrass them in front of their friends.

The hyperactive child is also likely to have social problems in the wider world of the neighborhood and the classroom. Although other children are not usually offended by high levels of activity, they are likely to be put off by the hyperactive youngster's impulsiveness and poor self-control. They dislike his rough, grabby behavior, his bossiness, and his inability to await his turn or abide by the rules of a game. They know him to be a poor loser and view his emotional outbursts with disdain. If he tends to blow up or burst into tears over minor upsets, other children are likely to ridicule him as a crybaby and may even take malicious pleasure in trying to provoke an outburst.

If the hyperactive child also has learning difficulties, his status with peers is further reduced. In a competitive society such as ours, in which personal worth is often confused with personal accomplishment, the child who can't keep up academically is seen by his classmates as inferior and worthless as a person. In the elementary school years, especially, children are quick to notice such deficiencies. Sadly, they are just as quick to point them out. "You can't even read *that?*" they taunt. "We learned that stuff last year. You must be stupid." If the child is in a special class, the treatment he receives from children in regular classes may be particularly harsh. I recall the horror with which one teenager received the news that his younger brother was going to be placed in a special class. "Are you crazy? You can't do that to him," he insisted to his parents. "They'll call him a 'sped' [for "special education"], and the way they treat speds—it's awful!"

Whether or not he has learning problems, the hyperactive child can be expected to gain greater control over his hyperactive, impulsive behavior as he matures. Unfortunately, he may still have difficulty making and keeping friends. While temper tantrums and "bouncing off the walls" diminish, other handicaps—less obvious but no less important—remain.

In particular, hyperactive children often seem completely unaware of the signals and cues that regulate social behavior. These cues, which often involve nonverbal behavior such as facial expression, posture, and gesture, are subtle, but they play a very important role in social exchanges. In a conversation between two people, for example, words carry only about one third of the total "message." The rest is conveyed through nonverbal signals like eye contact and facial expression. Obviously, the person who fails to detect these crucial signals is likely to completely misinterpret the message.

Because the hyperactive individual is not skilled at "reading" social signals, others often see him as eccentric, self-centered, and boorish. Failing to detect that others are bored or annoyed, he may talk too much, carry a joke too far, or insist on continuing an activity long after others in the group have tired of it.

Although Teddy was a bright, creative child who loved fantasy play, he seldom had companions to share the imaginative games he invented. A *Star Wars* buff, he initially impressed his classmates with his knowledge of plots and characters and his extensive collection of *Star Wars* toys. At first, they participated with enthusiasm in *Star Wars* games with him. When their fascination waned with time and their interest turned to other activities, Teddy seemed not to notice. GI Joe became the "in" toy around which playground games revolved, but Teddy continued to insist, "Let's play *Star Wars*." Annoyed with his single-mindedness, the others began to exclude him. Exclusion turned to active rejection, and by the end of the year Teddy was looked upon as a social outcast.

A common social handicap among hyperactive individuals is their insensitivity to the feelings of others. They may laugh at inappropriate times, tease in a hurtful way, and blurt out tactless remarks, completely unaware that they have given offense.

When Bill's younger brother brought his fiancée home to meet the family, Bill greeted his prospective sister-in-law with warmth. During the course of the evening, Bill learned that the young woman had been married before. "Oh, used goods, huh?" he joked. He was baffled by the stony silence that followed this remark.

Many hyperactive individuals—adults as well as children—find it hard to see how their own behavior contributes to their difficulties with others. Because they see only their own wants and needs and not the reactions of those around them, they often feel that they are misunderstood victims. "But I was only kidding!" is a familiar cry, as is "He started it. I wasn't doing anything at all." Even when his role in a situation is carefully explained to the hyperactive individual, he may stubbornly insist that he was not at fault and continue to blame others for his difficulty.

We don't know why people with ADHD are so often insensitive to social cues. Are they so inattentive that they overlook these subtle points? Or are they simply unable to "read" these cues, no matter how hard they concentrate? We know that hyperactive children often have difficulty in perceiving other aspects of the physical world accurately. These perceptual problems, which are frequently associated with learning disabilities, may also affect the hyperactive individual's ability to perceive his social world, as well as the world of letters and numbers.

We know, too, that insensitivity to social cues and a disregard for the social niceties can follow damage to the frontal lobes of the brain. Since this area of the brain has been pinpointed as the most likely site of brain malfunction in ADHD, it suggests that there is a physical cause for gaps in the hyperactive person's social skills.

Helping the Hyperactive Child with Social Problems

If your hyperactive child has a hard time making friends, you've shared the pain of his social rejection. You've probably experienced a host of other emotions, too: impatience with the child himself for being so inept socially, helpless rage at the classmates who taunt and tease, and a nagging worry that he will never find friends or fit in.

No doubt you've tried and tried to help your child make and keep friends. How often have you counseled, "Just ignore them when they tease you"? How many times have you explained why others object to his behavior? "The other kids think you're too bossy. You can't always be the one to decide what everyone will do. You have to let the others have a say, too."

It's a safe bet that your efforts have met with very limited success. What else can you do? The first step is to stand back and analyze the problem carefully. What does your child do that brings him into conflict with his peers or causes them to reject him? Does his rough, aggressive behavior intimidate other children? Is he so bossy and pushy that others steer clear of him? Is he a show-off who always demands, "Look at me!"? Perhaps he is so unfocused that he can't participate in games for more than a few minutes. Or it may be that other children are tired of putting up with his tears and angry outbursts when he loses a game.

Whatever the problem, if it seems to stem from poor impulse control and/or inattentiveness, it is quite likely that medication can help (see Chapter 4). Medication can also reduce the child's aggressive behavior—his tendency to punch first and ask questions later. Research has shown clearly that no other form of treatment—neither social skills training, behavior modification, nor psychotherapy—produces results comparable to those obtained with medication.

But medication helps only by decreasing behavior that is *antisocial* in nature. Since it does nothing to promote *prosocial* kinds of behavior, it is often only a partial solution to the hyperactive child's social problems. What else can you do to help?

• *Help your child improve his play skills.* If the child does not know the rules of the games his classmates like to play, teach him. If he lacks the necessary skills—if he can't throw or catch a ball, jump rope, or ride a bike—practice with him. If you lack the skill or the patience, find someone else who can teach him. The coach at the local high school might be able to recommend a high school athlete who would be interested in earning extra money by coaching your child.

• *Plan activities that are attractive to other children.* In order for other children to learn to like your child, they must first get to know him. You can encourage this by planning activities that children enjoy and inviting a classmate or a neighbor child to go along. Trips to the theater, amusement parks, and sports events are fun for children, as are swimming parties, movies, and dinner at your child's favorite fast food restaurant. Parties and sleepovers are also a good idea. Be sure to provide things that children enjoy, such as popular board games, video games, and lots of favorite foods. By making your child's company valuable to other children, you are creating opportunities for him to make friends and learn to get along with others.

• *Help your child learn new skills and develop new interests.* There are few sights more disturbing to a parent than a child who spends most of his time alone, slumped in front of a television. This, of course, does nothing to improve his self-concept or his social skills. Don't let your child become a "couch potato." Look for activities that will give your child a feeling of mastery and accomplishment. Lessons of almost any kind are excellent for this purpose, and the list is as long as your imagination: painting, dancing, tennis, karate, guitar, skating, acting, horseback riding, and so on.

Don't overlook church youth groups and scouting as sources of new interests and new friends. If your child resists the idea of joining such a group, his reluctance can often be overcome if you become a den parent or a youth group leader.

Teachers who have socially isolated hyperactive children in their classrooms can help, too. In some ways, this is an easier task for a teacher than a parent because a teacher does not have to create opportunities for the child to interact with other children: in a class of thirty children, these opportunities are ready-made. Suggestions for teachers are given in Chapter 8.

8

How Can We Reach Him to Teach Him?

The Hyperactive Child in School

THE SCHOOL'S ROLE IN DIAGNOSIS

Many hyperactive children are not diagnosed until they enter school, where they are faced with the academic and social demands of the classroom. In fact, most hyperactive children who are placed on medication do not begin taking medication until they enter elementary school at the age of five or six, even though they might have been seen earlier by a physician for behavior problems.

As a child goes from preschool to elementary school, he meets steadily increasing demands on his ability to organize himself, sit still, follow directions, and concentrate for long periods of time. A number of hyperactive children are identified for the first time in preschool, especially if they are aggressive and disobedient as well as overly active. However, because preschool is relatively unstructured and usually lasts only a few hours a day, some hyperactive children escape detection. First grade places much greater demands on the child to sit quietly and participate in teacher-directed activities. This is a peak period during which hyperactive children are identified as having problems and are referred for help. Another peak time comes in the third grade, when reading difficulties become increasingly apparent. By this time, too, children are expected to work independently and teachers are less tolerant of restlessness, daydreaming, and "off-task" behavior.

There are also some hyperactive children who are not referred for help until they reach junior high school, where they must cope with changing classes and reduced teacher support and supervision. Typically, although these children have consistently had problems through elementary school, parents and teachers have attributed their difficulties to immaturity. In many cases the child has repeated one or more grades in elementary school, in the hope that he would outgrow his problems and settle down. Finally, when the child's problems are still apparent in adolescence, a decision is made to seek help. In the meantime, of course, the child has fallen further and further behind academically, has suffered through years of failure and social rejection, and has usually developed a very poor self-image.

Whether a child is identified as possibly hyperactive can depend a great deal on such factors as the number of students and whether or not there are teacher's aides. The hyperactive child exists not in a vacuum but in a series of specific settings, and we know that his behavior can vary dramatically, depending on the setting in which he finds himself. For example, while many hyperactive children are indistinguishable from other children in free-play situations, they tend to stand out in more "formal" settings. In classrooms where children are allowed to select activities and work at their own pace, hyperactive children stand out less from their classmates than in classrooms where they must remain seated while doing assigned work or listening to the teacher present material. In the latter type of setting, unmedicated hyperactive children daydream more, make more strange noises, and move about more. Consequently, they are more likely to be labeled problem children by their teachers.

Of course, it's the teacher who sets the tone and style in the classroom, and the teacher's tolerance level and skill in working with hyperactive youngsters are critical factors in how well the hyperactive child fares in school. The teacher's role vis-à-vis these children is discussed in the next section.

GUIDELINES FOR TEACHERS

THE TEACHER-CHILD RELATIONSHIP

Next to his relationship with his parents, a child's relationships with his teachers are usually the most significant associations he has with adults during his childhood and adolescence. On numerous occasions, I have seen a remarkable improvement in a hyperactive youngster's behavior, schoolwork, self-esteem, and general outlook on life when he has been placed with a teacher with whom he "clicks." Unfortunately, the reverse is also the case: I have seen many hyperactive children take a sharp turn for the worse during school years in which the fit between teacher and child was poor.

Interviews with hyperactive teenagers and young adults conducted by Doctors Gabrielle Weiss and Lily Hechtman at Montreal Children's Hospital underscore the importance of the teacher-child relationship. Asked to look back over their early years, some of the interviewees reported very positive experiences with certain teachers, and several described these relationships as turning points in their lives. Some of the specific comments were:

"Mrs. X liked me; she used her free time to work with me and got me interested in math."

"Mr. B was the turning point of my life; it is hard to tell you how much he did for me."

Other interviewees recalled harmful experiences with teachers whom they felt disliked them, shamed them, or in other ways made life unpleasant for them. Typical comments were:

"Many of the teachers I had put me down and made me feel stupid."

"My homeroom teacher did not want me in her class and made it very obvious."

"One teacher had it in for me; I think he really hated me."

The Teacher's View. Of course, it is easy to understand how a hyperactive child might antagonize his teachers and bring out the worst in them. Just as a hyperactive child can exhaust the most loving of parents with his restless, impulsive, demanding behavior, he can also drain the most dedicated of teachers. In a class of thirty children, the child who makes strange noises, interrupts constantly, is always out of his seat, and demands help with the simplest tasks can drive a teacher to despair. Consider the following classroom observations made by the guidance counselor of a nine-year-old hyperactive boy.

9:55　Mrs. Mather is explaining a math problem to the class. Arnie is playing with something in his desk. Now he's looking at some papers in his social studies folder. Mrs. Mather asks, "Arnie, are you paying attention?" Arnie says, "What?"

10:00　Arnie is playing with a pencil, tapping his desk and rolling the pencil around on his desk. Mrs. Mather calls Arnie and two other children to come to the back of the room to sign up for science projects. He goes to the bulletin board and signs up.

10:05　The other children return to their seats. Arnie returns but does not sit down. He walks over to another boy and asks if he has signed up yet.

10:10 Arnie is standing next to his desk, looking around the room. Mrs. Mather comes over and tells him to get back to work. Arnie says, "I *am* working. I don't know how to do these problems" (the ones Mrs. Mather has just explained to the class). Mrs. Mather goes over a problem with him, checks the ones he has done, and tells him to redo a couple of them. She leaves. He looks around the room.

10:15 Arnie calls out, "Mrs. Mather." She says, "I asked you to redo those problems." Arnie says, "I did. I still don't understand." Mrs. Mather points out something on his paper, and he starts to work, still standing beside his desk. Now he's staring at a pen, playing with it, looking around the room. He starts to hum.

10:20 He's rooting through his desk, looking for something. He walks across the room toward the door. As he passes one boy, he pokes him. The other boy looks annoyed and says, "Stop it, Arnie." Arnie laughs. He walks out of the room, down the hall, and back, just looking around. He stands near his desk, looking around. He's tapping on his desk with his fingers, still humming.

10:25 He's dancing and appears to be trying to make some kids laugh. He walks over and looks at what another boy is working on. He tries to grab the other boy's paper. Mrs. Mather notices and says, "Arnie, please go back to your seat and do your work." He goes to his desk and begins to look for something in his backpack. Now he's searching his desk—now his backpack again.

10:30 Mrs. Mather tells the class to take out their spelling folders. Arnie is still looking in his backpack. Papers are scattered on his desk and on the floor. Mrs. Mather waits for Arnie, then asks him, "Do you have your spelling folder?" Arnie appears agitated and yells, "I can't find it!" Mrs. Mather comes over to help.

A hyperactive child like Arnie hits a teacher where it hurts most—right in the ego. As a teacher, your professional self-esteem depends to a great extent on how well your students respond to you. The hyperactive child threatens your competence because he threatens your ability to keep control in your classroom. You may feel that, if you can't control his unruly behavior, you will look foolish in front of your other students and in the eyes of your colleagues. You probably worry, too, that his behavior will have a bad influence on the other children, producing a ripple effect. You may be concerned about the fact that he distracts the other children from their work. If the hyperactive child is aggressive, you may even fear for the physical safety and well-being of the other children in your class.

It is certainly true that these children produce anxiety in teachers. Sally Smith, founder and director of the well-known Lab School in Washington, D.C., agrees. She adds, "When teachers are anxious, they become more tense, more demanding, more punitive, more scattered, more clumsy, less patient, less humorous, less sensitive, less organized, less confident. Anxiety can wear out the best of teachers and reduce effectiveness."[30]

Research supports these observations. In one study of hyperactive youngsters, researchers found that not only did teachers give more commands, punishment, and negative feedback to hyperactive children; this negative "set" also seemed to spill over into the teacher's interaction with other children in the class. In classrooms where there was a hyperactive child, the teacher interacted in a more negative fashion with the other children in the class, as well as with the hyperactive child.

The Child's View. Teachers often find that one of the most infuriating qualities of the hyperactive child is his general

inability to see how his own behavior contributes to his difficulties with others. When confronted with misbehavior, he
tends to blame everything and everyone else for the problem.
His stock replies are usually "It's not fair," "It wasn't my
fault," and "I didn't do anything."

We can begin to make sense of this baffling behavior if we
look at how the hyperactive child sees his own behavior and
how he interprets his teacher's reactions to him. These questions were explored in an intriguing study of how children
interpret the actions of their teachers and classmates. In this
study, conducted by Dr. Mary Rohrkemper at Michigan State
University, elementary school children were given fictional
examples of classroom misbehavior.[31] One example depicted
a child engaging in restless, hyperactive behavior, disturbing
other children in the class. After each example, the children
were asked, "Why did the child behave that way?" They were
also asked, "What would your teacher say to him if he acted
that way in her class?" and "Why would she say that?"

The results, summarized in Figure 9, provide a valuable
insight into the way the hyperactive child interprets his own
behavior and that of others toward him. The interpretations
given by hyperactive children differed strikingly from those
given by other children. Nonhyperactive children believed
that the fictional hyperactive child *could* control his behavior,
while hyperactive children believed that he *could not*. Both
groups predicted that the teacher would respond negatively
to such behavior, but, while other children interpreted the
teacher's behavior as simply "doing her job," hyperactive
youngsters saw her reactions as stemming from personal dislike of the child.

These findings help to explain the defensive behavior of the
hyperactive child. As Dr. Rohrkemper points out, hyperactive
children "apparently do not believe that they are in control of
their behavior. Thus, the negative reactions of teacher and
classmates likely appear unfair . . . (because it is obviously

	Non-ADHD Children	ADHD Children
Reason for behavior "Why did the child behave that way?"	Believed fictional character *could* control his behavior; blamed him for his own actions ("He does it because he wants to bother other kids").	Believed character *could not* control his behavior; blamed outside forces ("His friends bug him all the time") or other forces beyond character's control ("Her brain just goes too fast").
Predicting teacher's reaction "What would your teacher say to him if he acted that way in her class?"	Predicted negative reaction ("Punish him," "Tell him to stop it").	Predicted negative reaction ("Punish him," "Tell him to stop it").
Interpretation of teacher's reaction "Why would she say that?"	Concern for others in the class ("She's worried that others won't be able to get their work done"); teacher's role ("Because that's part of being a teacher").	Lack of concern for students ("She just likes to be the boss"); personal dislike of student ("She thinks he's a bad boy").

Figure 9. How hyperactive children interpret events in the classroom.

unfair to punish someone for something beyond his control).''

In this light, the hyperactive child's defensive reactions
make sense. From his point of view, he is not out to get you:
you are out to get *him*. He doesn't understand that you are
concerned about the welfare of the group: he thinks you simply dislike him. He cannot see that part of your responsibility
as a teacher is to keep some semblance of order in your
classroom: he believes that you just enjoy being a tyrant.

How can you help the hyperactive child understand how his
behavior affects others and why they react to him as they do?
Dr. Rohrkemper suggests that teachers can help by telling the
child how others interpret his behavior and by explaining the
rationale for their own behavior to the child. For example:

"When you wiggle around in your seat, it bothers the children near you. They can't finish their work. They think you do
it on purpose to bother them, so sometimes they get mad at
you. I'm not mad at you: I know it's hard for you to sit still.
Maybe if you sit up here next to me, that will help you sit and
do your work."

"I know you didn't mean any harm, but the rule is 'No
touching others when you walk by.' Poking other people
makes them angry. They think you mean to hurt them. Sometimes it scares them, too, because you poke them harder than
you mean to. Please keep your hands in your pockets when
you walk across the room. Maybe that will help."

"If you make a lot of noise in the halls, it disturbs children
in other classes. Maybe they're right in the middle of taking a
big test or doing something else that's important to them.
Other teachers would be upset with me if I let my children
disturb their children. I think it would be better if you walked
here beside me, and I'll help you walk quietly."

This approach conveys your concern for the child. It can also help him gain some self-awareness and, at the same time, prevent misunderstandings between teacher and child.

Controlling Your Emotional Reactions. Before you can help the scattered, demanding, intrusive hyperactive child, you must have your own emotions under firm control. This is a tall order, for all of the reasons already discussed. But responding to such a child with anger or by blaming him or shaming him—these reactions only add to the child's problems and to yours. How can you keep calm and "centered" when you deal with a child who brings out all of your own fears of inadequacy?

First, remember that the behavior you find so annoying comes from the *disorder*, not from the child. Think of a physically handicapped child. Is the blind child "doing it on purpose"? Is the child in the wheelchair just "too lazy" to walk? Of course not. Just as these children do not choose to be handicapped, neither do children choose the invisible handicap of ADHD.

It's helpful, too, to use your own emotions as signals. When you find yourself feeling defensive or resentful toward the hyperactive child, these feelings are your cue to look beyond the immediate situation to the real source of your own discomfort. Perhaps the child's behavior threatens your own feelings of competence and adequacy. You may be telling yourself, "How awful that he's making me look like a fool" or "A good teacher would be able to handle this child. I must be incompetent." In these situations, it's important to get your ego out of the way so you can act with the child's best interests in mind. When you ask, "How can I help him out of this predicament?" rather than "Why is he doing this to me?" you are more likely to come up with useful answers.

Perhaps, too, you are "catching" the hyperactive child's own negative emotions, which, according to Sally Smith, are "very contagious": "When the teacher says, 'This child will never learn!' she has caught the child's own feelings of defeat. When she says, 'No matter what I try, it doesn't work,' she has caught his frustration. . . . When she says, 'He's impossible,' she reveals her feelings of total inadequacy, the same feelings the child has."[32]

By staying in touch with your own emotions, you can stay in touch with the child's feelings. By staying in touch with the child's feelings, you stand the greatest chance of reaching the child.

PROVIDING STRUCTURE AND FEEDBACK

The Importance of Structure. Because the hyperactive child cannot organize himself or his world, others must assume this responsibility for him. "Organization," observes Sally Smith, "is the lifeline, the safeguard, the medicine, and the key to learning for the child who is disabled by disorganization or disorder."[33] By establishing a time and a place for everything in the classroom, the teacher provides the structure the hyperactive child so desperately needs.

An excellent model of an organized, structured classroom is the special classroom at the National Institute of Mental Health for children who are participating in research programs there. Classroom teacher Christine Leibner employs a behavior management system in which the children earn points, in the form of play money, for appropriate behavior and are fined for inappropriate behavior (see Appendix A for a description of this system). A list of specific behavior for which points are earned and lost is posted in a conspicuous spot in the room.

In the child's work area, there is a designated place for every item the child uses in the classroom. The folder containing finished work, for example, belongs in a certain location, while the folder containing work to be done belongs in another spot. The children earn points for keeping all work materials where they belong and are fined for items out of place.

In this classroom, too, all instructions are absolutely clear and quite precise. For instance, with this group of impulsive hyperactive youngsters, a general directive like "Line up for lunch" would probably produce shoving, pushing, and pandemonium. Instead, Ms. Leibner instructs the children as follows: "Place your unfinished work in your work folder. (Pause.) Good. Now put the folder in the center of your desk. (Pause.) Okay. Stand up and push in your chairs—quietly. (Pause.) Very good. Now, Mr. ———, you may get in line at the door."

These are carefully paced, detailed instructions the hyperactive child can follow successfully. Such attention to detail is also important when giving the child directions concerning academic tasks. The teacher who issues a rapid-fire series of directives is sure to lose the hyperactive child in the process. This child needs to have directions stated clearly and simply, one at a time.

INSTEAD OF THIS: "Now it's time to put away your math books and take out your spelling books and a piece of paper. Put your name and the date in the upper right corner of the paper. Then turn to page sixteen in your spelling book and do the first ten words on the bottom of the page."

TRY THIS: "Please close your math books. (Pause to allow hyperactive child to follow instruction.) Good. Now put them in your desks. (Pause again.) Now please take out your spelling books. (Pause again.) And now take out a piece of paper." And so on.

It's important, too, with hyperactive children, to be sure that you have their full attention while directions are being given. It helps to stand directly in front of the child, perhaps touching his shoulder to help maintain eye contact and attention.

Using Feedback to Improve Behavior. The importance of feedback—especially positive feedback—in managing the behavior of the hyperactive child was discussed in Chapter 5.

Remember that, to be most effective in controlling behavior, feedback must be delivered immediately after a behavior occurs, dispensed frequently, and given for small steps toward improvement. Positive feedback conveys much more information to the child and is more effective and efficient than negative feedback.

Unfortunately, like all of us, teachers tend to be much too stingy with praise and approval and too generous in doling out criticism and negative feedback. In fact, when researchers went into classrooms to study rates of teacher approval and disapproval, the findings were rather dismal. They found that:

• Only during the first and second grades do teachers give more praise than criticism or correction.

• In every grade beyond the second, teachers give more negative feedback than positive feedback.

• Praise is given almost exclusively for academic performance ("Yes, that's the correct answer"), while criticism is given almost exclusively for inappropriate behavior ("Sit still," "Stop talking," "Pay attention").

• The amount of teacher approval dispensed for appropriate classroom behavior is virtually *nonexistent.*

Think about it. When was the last time you said: "I really like the way you're paying attention." INSTEAD OF: "Stop daydreaming and pay attention." "Jeff is working so hard on his arithmetic." INSTEAD OF: "Jeff, get to work." "Thank you for raising your hand." INSTEAD OF: "Stop interrupting."

Yet this state of affairs is little short of crazy in light of countless studies documenting the power of positive reinforcement. In study after study, the picture is absolutely consistent: when teacher approval goes up, inappropriate behavior goes down. Why, then, do teachers behave this way? One explanation is that disapproval often stops misbehavior on the spot, so teachers are immediately reinforced for using negative feedback. But since the effects of disapproval are usually temporary and do nothing to decrease misbehavior in the long run, this is a very shortsighted approach.

To help you remember to "accentuate the positive," you might want to try the method suggested for parents in Chapter 5. Using an index card divided into columns marked "Praise" and "Criticism," make a check in the appropriate column each time you praise or criticize the hyperactive child in your class. Each day, try to give a little more praise and a little less criticism.

As your behavior changes, so will the child's—sometimes dramatically. (In one report, for example, a hyperactive child's time on task jumped rapidly from 62 percent to 96 percent when the teacher switched from criticizing him for off-task behavior to praising him for on-task behavior.) Of course, as improvement occurs, it makes it easier for you to give more praise. There's a fringe benefit, too: research shows that you can expect a "spillover" effect to extend to other children in the class. In other words, when the rate of teacher approval increases, even children who are not the direct recipients of praise tend to show improvement in their behavior.

Of course, negative feedback can't be eliminated entirely— nor should it be, since the best behavior results when hyperactive children receive a combination of positive consequences for appropriate behavior and mild negative consequences for inappropriate behavior. When it is necessary to correct a child, the negative feedback should be delivered as quietly and as unobtrusively as possible.

An excellent way to do this is to use the "response cost" procedure described by Dr. Mark Rapport, a psychologist at the University of Rhode Island.[34] Dr. Rapport suggests using two wooden stands with flip cards attached. The flip cards are made from poster-board and are numbered consecutively from one to thirty. The larger of the two stands is for teacher use. It should be completely mobile, lightweight, and visible from anywhere in the classroom if placed on a desk or a chair. The smaller stand is placed on the corner of the child's desk.*

The child is told that he can earn a certain amount of free time (up to thirty minutes in Dr. Rapport's program) by working hard during work period. He is also told that the teacher will occasionally look up from her work to see if he is on task. If he is not working, the teacher will flip a card down and one minute of his free time will be lost.

Dr. Rapport has used this system with hyperactive children and reports excellent results. In one case, for example, a hyperactive child's time on task jumped from 27 percent to 94 percent in a matter of a few days. There were corresponding gains in academic productivity, from virtually no assignments completed to nearly 100 percent completed, with excellent accuracy. In another case, the response cost procedure led to similarly dramatic gains in number of problems completed, from no problems at all to 100 percent of problems completed, again with excellent accuracy.

Dr. Rapport's system has a lot to recommend it. Teachers find it simple, practical, and effective to use in a classroom setting. The results, in terms of behavioral improvement, are certainly well worth the effort. The time and money spent in constructing the stands are minimal, and they can be used year after year.

HELPING THE HYPERACTIVE CHILD WITH PEER PROBLEMS

Whether or not a child is accepted by his classmates can be a make-or-break factor in the child's attitude toward school. How can you help your hyperactive student gain social acceptance among his classmates? You can begin by reinforcing the other children for including the hyperactive child in their activities. With younger children, direct praise is effective. You might say, for example, "How nicely you're all playing together. Jimmy, I like the way you're sharing the trucks with

---

* An electronic version of this apparatus, called the Attention Training System, is available from Gordon Systems, Inc., 301 Ambergate Road, DeWitt, NY 13214.

———— [hyperactive child's name]." With older children more subtle expressions of approval are in order. When you see the hyperactive child working or playing with others, make positive comments about the activity and the participants. For example, if Ted is working cooperatively with his work group on an art project, you can comment on how well everyone is working together and how attractive the art project is. Single Ted out for particular praise for his efforts.

Based on findings from his research, psychologist James Barclay offers these additional suggestions:[35]

• Plan activities in which the socially rejected child can participate as an equal or even a superior with other children. For example, you might have the children put on miniplays, cast the hyperactive child in the hero role, and commend him for his brilliant acting. (Miniplays are a delightful teaching device that can be incorporated easily into the teaching of virtually any subject.)

• Plan activities that depend on mutual cooperation for success. One example is a spelling game in which members of the team each have a letter printed on a piece of paper. When a word is called out, members of the team must arrange themselves so that the word is spelled correctly. Teams then compete with each other to see who can be first to spell the word correctly.

• Whenever possible, assign choice classroom jobs, such as hall monitor or errand runner, to the hyperactive child. Because these coveted positions themselves bestow a certain amount of prestige, the typical practice of assigning them to the better students (who tend to be among the more popular children in the class) really constitutes a waste of classroom resources. By using these positions to reinforce even the smallest improvements made by the hyperactive child, you accomplish two objectives at the same time: you reinforce appropriate behavior and you confer higher social status on the child.

• Break up existing cliques. When forming groups to work on projects or for other activities, do not allow the children to form their own groups. Otherwise, the popular children will tend to stick together and the hyperactive child is apt to be ostracized. Organize the groups so that the hyperactive child is paired with one or two of the most popular children in the class because popularity tends to "rub off."

UNDERACHIEVEMENT AND LEARNING DISABILITIES

Learning difficulties and poor school performance are very common in hyperactive children. Overall academic achievement among these children is usually below normal, with as many as half to three quarters underachieving in at least two academic subjects. Compared with other children, the risk of school failure is about two to three times greater among hyperactive youngsters, and it is estimated that about half will be held back at least one grade by adolescence.

The academic difficulties seen in so many hyperactive children are not the result of a lack of intelligence. In fact, some hyperactive children who obtain IQ scores in the intellectually gifted range perform quite poorly in school. Nor is the hyperactive child's poor academic achievement simply the result of problems with attention and concentration because, for many of these children, even when attention and concentration improve in response to medication, there is no corresponding improvement in academic performance.

WHAT IS A LEARNING DISABILITY?

Is your child learning-disabled? There is probably about as much confusion surrounding the term "learning disability" as there is about the term "hyperactivity." The term "learning-disabled" refers to *children who fail to learn despite an apparently normal capacity for learning.* This means that not all children who perform poorly in school can be considered learning-disabled. For example, a child who fails to learn at the expected rate because he is blind, deaf, or paralyzed would not be considered learning-disabled, nor would we use this label for a child whose poor academic performance stemmed from a generally low level of intelligence (mental retardation). Other children excluded from this category are those with significant emotional problems that interfere with their ability to learn and those from severely disadvantaged backgrounds who have not been exposed to learning opportunities.

The National Advisory Committee on Handicapped Children of the United States Office of Education has developed the following definition of a learning disability: "Children with special [specific] learning disabilities exhibit a disorder in one or more of the basic psychological processes involved in understanding or in using spoken or written language. These may be manifested in disorders of listening, thinking, talking, reading, writing, spelling, or arithmetic. They include conditions which have been referred to as perceptual handicaps, brain injury, minimal brain dysfunction, dyslexia, developmental aphasia, etc. They do not include learning problems which are due primarily to visual, hearing, or motor handicaps, to mental retardation, emotional disturbance, or to environmental disadvantage."

By this definition, about 3–10 percent of children can be considered learning-disabled. Not all of these children also have ADHD; there are children with "pure" learning disabilities who do *not* have problems with attention, concentration, and impulsiveness. Conversely, not all hyperactive children have specific learning disabilities. Many do, however, and although the exact figures are not known, the number appears to be considerable, with estimates ranging up to 85 percent.

Like ADHD, learning disabilities seem to run in families. Research suggests that 25–40 percent of learning-disabled children have other family members with similar difficulties. Also like ADHD, learning disabilities seem to affect many more boys than girls. In learning-disabled children, too, there is often a history of difficult or complicated pregnancy and delivery, head injuries, infections, and exposure to toxins. The parallels between the two conditions suggest that learning disabilities and ADHD may stem from the same origins and that both conditions may reflect a brain malfunction.

TREATING LEARNING DISABILITIES AND LEARNING DIFFICULTIES

State laws vary concerning how far behind a child must be to be considered technically learning-disabled and therefore eligible for special services in the public school system. But whether or not your child can be considered learning-disabled under the law, if he is falling behind in school, a complete evaluation is in order and remedial help is needed. There are so many different types of treatment programs that parents can easily become confused. Unfortunately, few of these programs have been evaluated to determine which ones are more helpful than others or, indeed, whether any of them help at all.

Approaches to the treatment of learning disabilities can be divided into *indirect remedial methods* and *direct remedial methods*.

Indirect Remedial Methods. Indirect approaches are based on the belief that learning problems are caused by underlying perceptual problems, motivational problems, or attentional problems. Of the many indirect approaches, the best known are those which emphasize perceptual training, on the theory that learning-disabled youngsters suffer from perceptual problems—in visual perception, orientation in space, visual-motor coordination, and so on. Numerous perceptual training programs have appeared over the years, involving a variety of exercises designed to improve the child's perceptual abilities. Some of these programs, such as the well-known Frostig Program, involve training in discriminating various patterns, forms, and sounds. Others focus on physical exercises and balance training to improve sensory-motor development. One such approach, known as the Doman-Delacato "patterning" method, involves a complicated routine of crawling and other exercises which the originators claim actually alters the way the brain functions. This unusual approach received wide publicity some years earlier, but in 1968 several professional organizations, including the American Academy of Pediatrics, issued a joint public statement expressing doubt about its merit.

Other approaches that aim to correct or improve activity in the central nervous system are also of questionable value. This includes optometric training, a program of eye exercises and other perceptual exercises administered by some optometrists. The American Academy of Pediatrics has also issued a statement criticizing this approach.

How helpful are these methods? As several experts have noted, none of the perceptual training approaches have been adequately evaluated to determine whether or not they actually benefit learning-disabled youngsters. From the limited evidence that is available, these approaches do *not* appear to be helpful. This is hardly surprising, since learning disabilities are now believed to reflect language disorders rather than perceptual problems.

A second group of indirect remedial approaches emphasizes the importance of motivation as a factor in learning problems. Some psychoanalysts, for instance, think that a failure to learn in school really reflects a fear of knowledge (because the individual is afraid of knowing about his own inner impulses) and recommend psychotherapy. Behavioral psychologists, on the other hand, make no such interpretation: they simply assume that reading, like any other behavior, can be strengthened by reinforcement. Psychotherapy does not seem to result in academic gains, although it may help children in other ways. Nor does the behavior modification approach fare much better unless it is combined with efforts to teach children specific academic skills when these skills are lacking.

Yet a third indirect approach is based on the assumption that learning problems are caused by problems with attention and concentration. Undoubtedly, this notion has been fueled by the fact that learning difficulties are so often seen in hyperactive children. Although stimulant medication improves the attention of hyperactive children and can lead to small improvements in academic performance, medication alone is not sufficient if the child lacks the basic skills needed for the task, for instance, if his word attack skills are weak or he has not learned the multiplication tables.

Although some of these approaches have a certain offbeat appeal that has made them quite popular, the verdict at this time is "Not proven" and parents would do better to look to more direct approaches to help their underachieving youngsters.

Direct Remedial Methods. Direct approaches to treating learning problems focus on teaching and practicing the specific skills required for the task. For a child who has difficulty with arithmetic, for instance, this means identifying gaps in the child's basic math skills and in his knowledge of mathematical concepts. Faced with an arithmetic problem, can your child understand what he has to do? Can he read numbers and mathematical signs correctly? (Obviously, if a child confuses the signs "$+$" and "$-$" he cannot begin to solve the problem.) Can he copy and write numbers and mathematical signs? Can he align columns of numbers correctly, or do his numbers wander all over the page? Does he know how to do each of the operations involved in the problem? Does he know how to carry and borrow? Has he learned basic math facts, such as $2 + 2 = 4$? Does he understand basic mathematical concepts, such as the notion that when you subtract one number from another the result should be smaller than the number you started out with? A thorough evaluation is necessary to pinpoint your child's specific areas of weakness. Only then can remedial efforts begin.

Similarly, children with reading and spelling problems require a systematic evaluation of skills and knowledge before remediation is attempted. The phonetic ("sound-it-out") method of reading remediation is one of the very few methods that has been definitely shown to help youngsters with reading problems. Mastering the basics of phonetics is essential for reading-disabled children to improve their reading. Therefore, the evaluator should assess your child's word attack and word analysis skills. Does your child know the sounds of individual letters and letter combinations? Can he sound out an unfamiliar word? Does he comprehend what he reads?

If weaknesses are identified in any of these areas, the specific skills must be taught, preferably on an individual basis. Individual tutoring in reading appears to be more effective than group instruction, especially with severely delayed readers. With these youngsters, according to Dr. Rachel Gittelman of Columbia University, "group instruction is definitely inferior."[36]

SPECIAL PROGRAMS IN THE PUBLIC SCHOOLS

In the past, a child who was underachieving or actually failing in school despite apparent good intelligence was apt to be written off as immature, unmotivated, or simply lazy. A popular solution was to have the child repeat the grade. This strategy was seldom successful because, without a clear understanding of why he hadn't learned the first time around, the child was often doomed to fail a second time.

Since the passage of Public Law 94-142 in October 1975, the situation has changed considerably. This law, known as the Education for All Handicapped Children Act, removes the onus for failure to learn from the child and places responsibility on the school system to provide special services for children who need them. The law guarantees a free and appropriate education for all handicapped children between the ages of three and twenty-one—defined as those who are deaf, hard of hearing, visually handicapped, speech-impaired, seriously emotionally disturbed, orthopedically handicapped, otherwise health-impaired, and with specific learning disabilities—including:

• *Educational evaluation.* A comprehensive educational evaluation, including intelligence and achievement testing, must be provided by the public school system. The evaluation process can be initiated by either the parents or the school but cannot proceed without the parents' written permission. The evaluation must be administered by trained personnel, and the evaluation team must be multidisciplinary.

• *Individualized Educational Plan (IEP).* The IEP is a written plan detailing the program of instruction that will be provided to the child. Specifically, the IEP must include:

1. A statement of the child's current level of performance;

2. A statement of annual goals or achievements and short-term objectives;

3. A statement of the specific educational and related services to be provided for the child (related services provided at no cost to parents include transportation, speech therapy, occupational therapy, and the like);

4. The dates services will begin and the expected duration of each service;

5. A statement of evaluation procedures to determine whether objectives are being achieved.

• *Least restrictive environment.* In the past, handicapped children were usually segregated from nonhandicapped children in special classes or even separate schools. All too often, these special settings served as "dumping grounds," with little expected of the children in the way of achievement. Under Public Law 94-142, handicapped and nonhandicapped children must be educated together, to the extent that this is possible and appropriate. For example, some children with minimally handicapping conditions can remain in regular classrooms if they receive a couple of hours of special "resource" help each week. Other children simply cannot function successfully in a regular classroom setting and need the small class size and highly specialized teaching provided by a self-contained class-room.

The school system must provide a continuum of services, ranging from special resource help for handicapped children in regular classrooms to residential settings for severely hand-icapped youngsters. If a child requires services that are not available in the public school system, the school system must pay for the child's placement in an appropriate private facility.

• *Parent participation.* Parent participation in all aspects of a child's education is guaranteed under Public Law 94-142. Parents must, for instance, give written permission for their child to be evaluated. They must also be invited to participate in developing the IEP and must sign it before it can be imple-mented. Parents also have the right to review any and all records concerning their child.

Because Public Law 94-142 is potentially so important to hyperactive children who need special services in school, it is vital that parents be thoroughly familiar with the provisions of this law. However, parents cannot assume that, just because this law exists, their child's needs will automatically be served. Special education services are expensive, and school budgets are shrinking. Too often, the child with an "invisible handi-cap" is overlooked, even though the law guarantees him a free and appropriate education. The parents of such a child must not only be well informed; they must also be prepared to serve as the child's advocates.

Detailed information about Public Law 94-142 is discussed in two excellent books, both of which focus on learning-dis-abled children:

The Misunderstood Child: A Guide for Parents of Learning Disabled Children, Larry B. Silver, M.D., McGraw-Hill Book Com-pany, 1984

No Easy Answers: The Learning Disabled Child at Home and at School, Sally L. Smith, Bantam Books, 1981

Parents can obtain additional information from the following sources:

Closer Look, Parents' Campaign for Handicapped Children and Youth, P.O. Box 1492, Washington, DC 20013
Association for Children with Learning Disabilities, 4156 Library Road, Pittsburgh, PA 15234

HOME-SCHOOL COOPERATION

PARENTS AND TEACHERS HAVE DIFFERENT PERSPECTIVES

Because they see the child under such different circumstances, it is understandable that parents and teachers sometimes have very different perspectives on the hyperactive child. Certainly, a great many hyperactive children have difficulty both at home and in school. I have also encountered hyperactive youngsters whose behavior was in many ways worse at home than in school. (Often, these are bright, middle-class children who have been trained to respect adult authority and who have enough "social savvy" to avoid making spectacles of themselves in front of their peers.)

Usually, however, when parents and teachers see a child's behavior very differently, it is the teacher who has more complaints because the school setting highlights the child's weaknesses. This is especially true with a child whose parents are tolerant of active, exuberant behavior.

I am reminded of five-year-old Joey, whose parents brought him for an evaluation under pressure from the school system. They thought Joey was delightful. And he was. Magazine-cover cute, with shiny dark hair and enormous brown eyes, he was also friendly, verbal, and obviously quite intelligent. While I was admiring his charm, however, Joey was systematically demolishing my office. Finally, as several books came crashing from the shelves, I asked the parents, "Doesn't this kind of behavior bother you at home?" "Oh, no," Joey's mother assured me. "When he gets like this, I just open the back door and whistle." (She gave an ear-piercing demonstration.) "He goes out and runs around the yard for a couple of hours. When he comes back in, he's just fine."

It's easy to see that, in Joey's case, parents and teachers will have very different feelings about Joey's rambunctious behavior. The teacher finds it hard to believe that Joey isn't much of a problem at home. Joey's mother can't understand why the teacher is making such a fuss. From these very different perspectives, mistrust and animosity grow.

A WORKING ALLIANCE

How can parents and teachers avoid the trap of mutual blame and mistrust? As a teacher, you can help in the following ways:

• Respect the parent's point of view and knowledge of his or her child. You are an expert in the area of education, but the parent is an expert on the total child. By encouraging the parent to talk about the child's strengths and weaknesses, likes and dislikes, you can gain valuable information that will help you in working with the child.

• Remember that the parent has a tremendous emotional investment in the child. The parent will have responsibility for the child long after he or she has left your classroom. Therefore, the parent has much more to lose by the child's failure than you do. Because the parent has so much at stake, emotions are apt to run high. If the parent seems belligerent or defensive, try not to take it personally.

• Be sensitive to the fact that the parent is in a "one-down" position. Many adults who are otherwise quite competent and confident feel intimidated when they enter a school building. The sights and smells call up vivid memories of being a powerless child in a world where all power resides in teachers and principals. The anxiety these memories generate may be expressed as defensiveness or hostility. Again, don't take it personally.

• Remember to focus on the child's strengths as much as possible. This makes it easier for parents to accept your description of the child's weaknesses. When you describe the child's problems, choose your words carefully. Avoid judgmental labels like "irresponsible," "careless," and "sloppy." Talk only about what the child does or does not do, for example, "Jake does not turn in his homework." Don't interpret ("He's just not motivated") and don't blame ("You don't supervise his homework very closely").

Parents, too, must do their share to build a working alliance. As a parent, keep these points in mind:

• Try to understand the teacher's point of view. Behavior that is acceptable in the looser environment of your own home may be quite unacceptable in the classroom. Behavior that seems inconsequential to you may pose major problems in a class of thirty children.

• When a problem crops up between teacher and child, don't automatically side with your child. Remember that hyperactive children have great difficulty interpreting the behavior of others toward them and in understanding how their own behavior contributes to a situation. Therefore, your child's version of a situation may not be a very accurate account of what actually happened.

• Insist on the services your child needs but try to be realistic in your demands on the teacher. Hyperactive children often need special assistance to function successfully in school, but it need not always be the teacher who provides this assistance. For example, while some teachers can assume the responsibility for reminding the child to go to the nurse's office for his noon medication, others find it impossible to remember to do this regularly. If this is the case, work with the teacher, the guidance counselor, and other school personnel to develop a workable alternative.

• Remember that teachers need stroking, too. Express your appreciation for the teacher's efforts not only to the teacher, but to the principal. Better yet, take the time to put it in writing.

COMMUNICATION BETWEEN HOME AND SCHOOL

Although it is essential to keep open the lines of communication between home and school, this isn't always easy to accomplish. The busy schedules of parents and teachers may make frequent conferences difficult, if not impossible. A system of daily notes home from the teacher is helpful, but, in most cases, this simply is not possible. If notes are sent home only when there is a problem, the hyperactive child usually "forgets" to deliver the note to his parents.

Communicating by telephone offers an alternative, but here, too, there are drawbacks. Teachers usually cannot leave the classroom to hold telephone conversations, so scheduling telephone conferences can be problematic. Another problem arises when telephone calls are made to report a problem. Although parents need and want to be kept informed, if the teacher calls frequently to report misbehavior, the parent may become defensive as soon as he hears the teacher's voice on the other end of the line.

When there is need for very close communication between home and school, the best system is to use a brief, individualized checklist called a home-school report (see Figure 10). Parents and teachers can work together to target specific behavior like "Completing classwork" and "Quiet in cafeteria." The teacher initials the checklist daily and sends it home with the child. At home, you may wish to provide a backup system such as granting daily privileges based on your child's performance in school that day.

WINNING THE BATTLE OF THE HOMEWORK

Homework is probably the single biggest source of conflict between the school-age hyperactive child and his parents and teachers. To the parent, the process appears simple enough:

Figure 10. Home-school behavior report form.

Name _____

Behaviors	Dates									
1. _____										
2. _____										
3. _____										
4. _____										
5. _____										
6. _____										

Instructions to teacher _____

_____

_____

you bring home your assignments, complete the work, and turn it in the next day. In practice, the hyperactive child can stumble over any or all of the many steps involved in the homework process. For example:

• He does not write down the assignment. Consequently, he forgets what he is to do.

• He copies the assignment but doesn't understand what he is to do.

• If he understands the assignment and writes it down, he misplaces it somewhere between school and home.

• He forgets necessary books and materials.

• At home, he postpones and procrastinates as long as possible, approaching his work only after prolonged parental nagging and threats.

• Once at his desk, he daydreams, fiddles with objects, and does everything but the assigned work. Constant supervision is needed to keep him on task. He drags his homework out for hours.

• He rushes through his work, producing a product that is smudged, messy, and illegible.

• He doesn't check his work for errors, so the finished product is full of careless mistakes.

• Even when he has completed his assignments, he forgets to turn them in.

With so many pitfalls and problems, it's hard for parents and teachers to know where to begin.

Keep Track of Assignments. Since your child cannot possibly complete his assignments if he has no idea of what he is to do or if he lacks essential books and materials, keeping track of homework assignments is a crucial first step. Short of sending a private secretary to school with him each day, what can you and your child's teachers do to ensure that he will succeed in this area? Sometimes a simple behavior management program is enough: your child earns privileges like television time and outdoor play by bringing home his assignments and all necessary materials. If he fails to do so, he forfeits his privileges that day.

If this doesn't work, more intensive measures are in order. For the child who constantly forgets his books, it makes sense to purchase a second set of textbooks to be kept at home.

The problem of forgetting daily assignments is a thornier one. One solution is to use a buddy system, appointing one of the better-organized students in the class to act as your child's "secretary" and provide him with a written list of daily assignments. However, since the problem of forgetting daily assignments is such a common one among all children, teachers would do many of their students a big favor by providing weekly (better yet, *monthly*) assignment sheets that contain all assignments for the period. (I cannot understand why this is not standard practice in elementary schools and high schools:

in most college courses, students receive a syllabus detailing all assignments, quizzes, and tests for the entire semester!)

For longer-term assignments, such as science projects and book reports, ample notice is usually given, but the disorganized hyperactive child seldom plans his schedule accordingly. You can help by providing your child with a calendar on which these assignments can be recorded. This gives your child a much better idea of what "due in three weeks" means.

You can also help your child organize his work by providing separate folders or notebooks for different classes and by checking regularly to be sure that papers are in the correct folders. Before your child goes to bed on school nights, be sure that all materials needed for school the next day are organized and in a location where they will not be overlooked in the morning rush.

Organize Your Child's Work Area. A quiet, well-organized work area is a must for the hyperactive child. No child, least of all one with the hyperactive child's problems with attention and concentration, can do his best work sprawled in the family room surrounded by siblings, pets, and a blaring television set.

Your child should study in one location and one location *only.* Ideally, this should be a desk in his bedroom, although with children who initially require much supervision this may be a goal rather than a starting point. Whatever the location, it should be used for no other purpose than studying so that the child learns to associate that location with work. There should be no distracting objects within reach—no comics, no gerbil cages—just your child's work materials.

Structure Your Child's Time. Time management is extremely difficult for most hyperactive children. Having a set routine is essential, so it's wise to establish a routine for homework early in your child's school career.

It's important to set a time when homework is to begin each day and stick to that time. Parents often ask whether it is reasonable to expect a child to do his homework in the afternoons or if it would be better to let him have some free time before settling down to work. While after-school outdoor play is certainly desirable, allowing your child to play first and work later often results in procrastination and pitched battles late in the evening. If this is the case, he should be expected to begin his homework shortly after he arrives home from school. Only when he is performing acceptably on this schedule should you allow him to have another try at playing first and working later. If this is unsuccessful, return to the afternoon homework schedule.

Of course, many working parents cannot be home to supervise homework in the afternoons. In this case, the options are: (1) hire a reliable neighborhood teenager to monitor homework; or (2) have your child do his homework in the evening when you or your spouse can provide supervision.

The child should be seated at his workplace, ready to begin, at the established time. As a first step, your child should review his assignments for the day, estimate how much time each assignment should require, and plan the order in which he will tackle them. He should also review his long-term calendar and incorporate work on long-term projects into his work schedule. Obviously, all of this is a tall order for the hyperactive child, and he will initially require a great deal of assistance, but planning his time in this fashion not only helps him become more organized; it also makes the day's work seem more manageable. About ten to fifteen minutes should be allotted for planning time (probably more until the child gets the knack of it), after which you should ask to review the work plan.

Breaks should be scheduled at regular intervals. Just how long the child should work before taking a break depends on the individual child. Some children, especially younger ones, will need a break every fifteen minutes or so, while older children may need breaks less often.

How much time should a child devote to homework each day? In the early elementary grades, fifteen to thirty minutes should suffice. By about the fourth grade, your child should be spending about an hour or so daily doing homework, whether or not he has an assignment. (If he has no assignment, he can read, review, and work on long-term projects.) By the sixth grade, most schools require between one and two hours daily and, by high school, at least two hours.

If the time your child devotes to homework regularly falls far outside these rough limits—your fourth-grader, for example, spends three or more hours daily on homework, or your sixth-grader completes his work in fifteen minutes—something's wrong. The dawdler is probably wasting much of his time staring into space, while the speed demon is almost certainly producing sloppy, half-finished work. Knowing that he must remain at his desk for a certain period of time, regardless of whether he finishes early, helps slow down the speedster. This child will also benefit from learning to check his work for errors. The slowpoke, on the other hand, can benefit from methods that improve attention and concentration.

Maximize Attention and Concentration. Since schoolwork makes heavy demands on a child's ability to concentrate, most hyperactive children on stimulant medication will benefit from an afternoon dose of medication to help them focus on their homework. If you are reluctant to have your child on a third dose of medication, or if medication alone is not enough to keep your child on task, an "attention tape,"[37] suggested by Dr. Ted Glynn at the University of Auckland, New Zealand, may be helpful. To make an attention tape, you will need a tape recorder, a watch with a second hand, and a means of producing a soft but distinct tone (a table knife tapped gently against a water glass will do).

Start the tape, allow it to run for about fifteen seconds or so, and announce, "Begin." Using the numbers in the list for Tape 1 (below), sound the tone at intervals. The first tone is sounded one minute after you announce "Begin"; the second tone is sounded two minutes after the first; and so on.

TAPE 1	TAPE 2	TAPE 3
1	3	3
2	3	4
3	2	3
2	4	5
1	3	4
2	3	2
3	2	4
1		3
		2

When your child is ready to begin his work, he turns on the tape. As each tone sounds, he asks himself, "Was I paying attention to my work?" If he is able to answer "Yes," he makes a check in a "Yes" column on a sheet of paper. Otherwise, he makes a check in the "No" column.

Initially, it may be necessary for you to supervise this procedure, but as soon as possible the task should be turned over to your child. If self-monitoring is presented as an enjoyable challenge, most children will cooperate willingly. As your child's ability to stick to his work improves, more challenging tapes can be made by using the list for Tape 2 to produce a twenty-minute tape, then by using the list for Tape 3 to make a thirty-minute tape. By the time your child has advanced to the third tape, he should be able to focus on his work for periods of time adequate to complete his homework (allowing for breaks every half hour or so).

For the most part, children with whom I've used this method have found it helpful and fun. Parents agree that it does help children stay on task, so work is completed faster and more accurately.

Teach Proofreading. When teachers grade a child's written work, it is usually more than the thought that counts: they must take into account accuracy, neatness, and legibility. Even when the hyperactive child does turn in a completed assignment, he is often penalized for careless errors, poor penmanship, and misspelled words. Eventually, this can be so discouraging that many hyperactive children simply don't bother to turn in their papers.

Teaching your child to proofread his work and correct his own errors is important, but it isn't easy because, having labored to produce a piece of work, the child is apt to respond to critical comments and corrections with a temper tantrum. Making a game of catching his errors before the teacher does may help. It helps, too, to couch your corrections in positive terms. Even the messiest paper contains a paragraph—or even a sentence—that looks better than the rest of the work. Praise this portion of the work and challenge your child to make the rest of the work look just as good.

Use Incentives. Even for very bright hyperactive children, schoolwork is often a struggle. Generous amounts of praise and positive feedback for small steps toward improvement can go far in keeping your child on the right track. Remember to praise the behavior, though, not the child.

INSTEAD OF: "You're so smart."
SAY: "You worked so hard to make this neat. Good job."
OR: "I know this was a tough assignment but you stuck with it and I'm proud of you."

Schoolwork is one area in which caution about using material items to reinforce good performance can be relaxed a bit, if you use attractive school supplies as reinforcers. Most youngsters enjoy visiting office supply stores with their tempting displays of colored markers, bright folders, index cards, notepads, and so on. A supply of these special items can make homework seem a bit less boring and a bit more like fun.

Appendix

Behavioral Management Programs for Classroom Use

Christine Leibner, M.Ed., Special Educator, Montgomery County Public Schools and the National Institutes of Health

Janet Amass, B.S., C.L.S., Therapeutic Recreation Specialist, The National Institutes of Health

When hyperactive adults are asked to recall what was most helpful to them as children in overcoming their difficulties, the most common response tends to be of one particular teacher or person who believed in them or in the development of a particular talent. Describing what caused them the greatest difficulty, many reply "feeling dumb" and "being criticized."

From this, it would seem that positive and enriching educational experiences are particularly important for hyperactive children. In fact, one group of experts states flatly, "The importance of teachers and their classroom programs *cannot be underestimated* in the life of the child considered hyperactive."

Unfortunately, these children are often difficult and frustrating to teach. Teachers complain, too, that they are often kept in the dark by parents and health professionals, thus compounding their problems with the children themselves. Specifically, teachers complain of inadequate information about drug effects and side effects and disagreements between parents and physicians regarding treatment plans. Most teachers need and want to increase their involvement in the overall care of problem children. Not only should they be kept informed of their students' medical and psychosocial status; they should also become integral participants in the care of the whole child.

This appendix describes behavior management techniques designed for application in the regular classroom and is meant to enhance the quality of teacher-child relationships and to influence academic and social behavior. Detailed explanations are presented of three intervention programs developed at the National Institute of Mental Health. Their effectiveness is based on more than five years of clinical use with hyperactive children in this setting. However, because every teacher-child relationship is unique, we make no claims to have developed strategies for all cases in all settings. Hyperactive children must be approached on an individual basis. The intervention techniques described here are intended to serve simply as models.

MODELS OF MANAGEMENT

MODEL 1: THE CURRENCY-BASED TOKEN ECONOMY

In the Currency-based Token Economy (CBTE), students earn tokens for appropriate behavior and can use these tokens to purchase a variety of reinforcers. The tokens in CBTE are play money or "counterfeit" bills in denominations equivalent to those in U.S. currency. This system provides for immediate exchange, an element which is critical in making it an effective behavior management tool. With this system, the child earns at a very high rate, so appropriate behavior can be reinforced frequently. The child saves his earnings and uses them to purchase reward items on a weekly (or, in some cases, daily) basis.

Some of the behaviors for which the child earns bills are:

- Appropriate hands/hands in place ($5)
- Chair and desk in order ($5)
- Completing classroom assignments ($5–$25)*
- Completing homework assignments ($5–$25)*
- Following directions ($10)
- Keeping to one's self ($15)
- On-task behavior ($10)
- Participation ($15)
- Politeness ($10)
- Positive response/compliance ($15)
- Promptness ($25)
- Raising hand ($10)
- Staying seated ($10)
- Sitting still ($10)
- Walking/not running ($10)

Children are fined for inappropriate classroom behaviors, including the following:

- Argumentative response ($10)
- Incomplete classroom assignment ($5–$25)*
- Incomplete homework assignment ($5–$25)*
- Chair tipping, desk tipping ($5)
- Chair and desk out of order ($5)
- Disrupting others ($15)
- Inappropriate hands ($5)

- Late for
  school   (20)
- Negative re-
  sponse/non-
  compliance   ($10)
- Out of seat   ($20)
- Nonparticipa-
  tion   ($10)

- Off-task be-
  havior   ($10)
- Playing with
  money   ($15)
- Talking out   ($10)
- Running   ($10)

* Amount depends on quality and quantity of work.

The frequency with which the designated amounts are earned may vary according to the teacher's expectations for individual children. For instance, the child who has learned to stay seated will earn less frequently for this behavior than the child who is constantly out of his seat and still requires frequent reinforcement for staying in his seat.

When a fine is issued, if the child's current bank account is insufficient to pay the fine, he is issued an IOU. Once he has earned the amount needed to repay the IOU, he is cleared by the bank and resumes saving.

Children keep their earnings in "bank pouches" made from large envelopes. The bank pouch is kept in a designated position on the child's desk to facilitate access, which is essential for effective exchange. When it is not in use (e.g., during lunch or recess), the bank pouch is placed in the "bank safe," a secure area accessible only to the teacher. This avoids the risk that children will be tempted to abuse the system in any way, and it allows the teacher to monitor how much the child is earning.

Earnings are cashed in to purchase reinforcers during a specific period of time set aside each week. If a weekly schedule is too infrequent to maintain a high level of motivation, as may be the case with younger or more immature children, a more frequent schedule can be used initially.

Reward items may differ according to each child's individual interests. Thus, children should be allowed to choose reward items that are apt to be the most motivating. Sometimes a child has difficulty selecting a reward and needs a list of items from which he can choose. Rewards available in our program include:

- Academic games
- Serve as "banker," room monitor, messenger
- Errand person
- Calendar assistant
- Book reading
- Field trips
- Outside play
- Reading group leader
- Library time
- Computer time
- Puzzle time
- Free time
- Map reading
- Stickers
- No homework
- Books or maps for home

In this model, as in the others, Time Out is used if fining the child proves ineffective. Continual disruptive behavior and aggressive behavior warrant Time Out, a procedure which removes the child from all forms of attention and from the opportunity to earn currency. The procedure we use for Time Out is explained fully in a later section.

MODEL 2: THE HAPPY FACE REINFORCER

This model provides another method of changing behavior through the use of consequences. It is similar to the CBTE in its influence on specific behaviors but differs in that, although immediacy is still crucial, the rate of exchange is less frequent. In the NIMH program, Happy Face (HF) discs are used during recreation, when social behavior is the central focus.

Social and group behaviors for which children earn HF discs include the following:

- Allows others to complete statements (3)
- Keeps hands at side or on task (1)
- Initiates cleanup (3)
- Keeps shoes tied (1)
- Listens to and follows directions (3)
- Looks at speaker/eye contact (3)

- Shares information in
  polite tone   (3)
- Speaks clearly   (2)
- Talks about himself   (4)
- Tells the truth   (4)

- Waits in line   (2)
- Waits for turn   (2)
- Walks in halls   (1)
- Compliments a peer   (4)

Children lose HF discs for infractions of social and group rules, as follows:

- Lies to avoid blame   (4)
- Works without direc-
  tions   (3)
- Interferes with oth-
  ers' work   (3)
- Interrupts speaker   (2)
- Uses bossy or de-
  manding voice   (3)
- Mumbles or whines   (2)
- Avoids eye contact   (3)

- Runs or skips in hall   (1)
- Runs ahead of group   (1)
- Shoelaces untied   (1)
- Leaves group without
  permission   (4)
- Teases   (4)
- Grabs or shoves   (3)
- Tattles   (2)
- Hands on others   (2)

A place is designated for the accumulation of HF discs. Although the place will vary with the setting of activities, discs must always be available for exchange. Ideally, an area in the child's workplace is set aside as a savings location. At other times a jar, a shoebox, or the child's pocket serves as a savings area. In any event, the HF discs are not to be handled except during exchange from teacher to child or child to teacher.

A constant barrage of positive comments from the teacher accompanies and supplements the distribution of HF discs. These comments express pleasure over the positive interactions occurring in the group and outline *why* certain behaviors are appropriate and pleasing. Such comments boost the self-esteem of the children and contribute to the continuation of appropriate patterns of social behavior.

Over time, the frequency of positive reinforcement is gradually decreased. Children continue to accumulate reinforcement for the same behaviors but require less of it to keep their behavior on track. The child's progress itself comes to serve as a reinforcer as, for example, he can see that where he could once spend only five minutes in a group before a problem occurred, he has now progressed to twenty minutes. Children are encouraged to share their pride in these accomplishments with others in the group. The teacher can help by describing and praising these achievements to other children in the group and to other adults in the environment.

HF discs can be exchanged according to a purchasing schedule which best fits the needs of the child and the teacher. Ultimately, a weekly exchange is the goal. Some children need a more frequent exchange in the beginning to reinforce their efforts. Reinforcers, like those used in the CBTE, are intangible and many provide an opportunity for enhancing self-esteem by providing a prestigious position within the group. Examples of reinforcers used in our program include:

- Distribution and collection of equipment
- Act as helper
- Use of musical instruments
- Use of tape recorder
- Puzzle time
- Reading time
- Use of art supplies
- Quiet games (dominos, lotto)

MODEL 3: CONTRACTS

The concept of individual contracts can also be employed in the regular classroom. With this system, specific problem behaviors, identifiable by both child and teacher, are outlined. Because the contract clearly outlines the requirements of both parties, it is designed to avoid arguments over interpretation. Both child and teacher agree to take a role in planning the contract, so each is an active participant. All sections of the contract are negotiated and mutually agreed upon.

Sample Contract

Contract for: Mitchell

The problem is: Touching others in line

To help myself: I will stay at one arm's length from the
   person in front of me

Others can help by: Touching my shoulder lightly if I get
   too close

I am earning towards: One transformer

Signed: _____ _____
            (Child)   (Teacher)

In negotiating the contract, the child has an opportunity to request both the type of assistance he needs in order to attain his goal and the reinforcer he would like to earn by achieving his goal. The child selects reinforcers he considers motivating, and the teacher outlines the behavioral limits. It is necessary for the teacher to ensure a successful initial experience so that the child feels encouraged and highly motivated. The collaborative nature of the contract as well as its success-oriented framework often results in immediate improvement in the child's self-esteem.

In this process, it is vital that all problem behavior be spelled out in *specific* and *positive* terms. For example:

INSTEAD OF: "I want Bill to stop being so sloppy" (negative, unclear statement of goal)

STATE: "Bill is to stack his finished work and books to the right of his desk at lunchtime" (clear, positive statement of goal)

The teacher may discover that some behaviors are eliminated in a mutually exclusive fashion; e.g., if "out of seat" and "disturbing others while they work" are both problem behaviors, both may be reduced if the child's goal is "to remain seated." The teacher can point this out to the child, and the child can feel doubly successful as he eliminates both behaviors simultaneously.

Contracts are particularly useful with children who need

practice in problem-solving skills. They are also helpful with children who act impulsively and who are constantly sorry for the aftermath of their impulsive actions, e.g., tardiness, knocking over equipment, crashing into others.

The interval between the behavior and delivery of the reinforcer should be no longer than one week. Again, as with Models 1 and 2, younger children may need reinforcement more frequently.

How many specific target behaviors should be included in a single contract? Children younger than eight years of age can usually manage no more than one target at a time. Children eight years and older are more often capable of contract agreements listing several behaviors targeted for change at the same time.

USING THE MODELS SUCCESSFULLY

In all three models, a key component in bringing about change is that target behaviors are specific, positive, and attainable. The cost of reinforcers should be gradually increased over time as the child becomes proficient. Simultaneously, praise should replace tangible reinforcers for behaviors that have been satisfactorily modified through use of the behavior management system. As the child's classroom behavior becomes more acceptable to the teacher, different target behaviors are introduced.

For the child with difficulty in organization, poor impulse control, poorly modulated moods, and excessive need for teacher attention, a predictable and consistent environment is critical. Using the approaches we have outlined, lecturing becomes unnecessary. Enforcement occurs in a controlled, unemotional manner that does not assault the child's dignity or self-esteem. In fact, the child's confidence and self-esteem increase as he learns that, on each and every occasion, the same behavior leads to the same outcome. Therefore, although praise is given for effort, "almosts" are not rewarded.

INTERVENTIONS FOR SPECIFIC PROBLEM BEHAVIORS

The following guidelines suggest methods for managing specific problem behavior, using Models 1, 2, and 3.

• *Problem:* Talking without permission (classroom); interrupting others

Models 1 and 2: Issue a fine of $10 (Model 1)/1 HF disc (Model 2). In a neutral tone and manner, describe the rule violation and the fine: "There is a fine of $10 for talking in this classroom" or "There is a fine of 1 disc in this group for interrupting others."

Model 3: A precise, positive way of describing this behavior in the child's contract is "I wait until I am recognized before speaking. I wait until others are finished before I speak."

• *Problem:* Leaving seat without permission

Models 1 and 2: Issue a fine of $20 (Model 1)/2 HF discs (Model 2). In a neutral tone and manner, describe the rule violation and the fine: "There is a fine of $20 for being out of seat in this classroom" or "You are fined 2 HF discs for leaving your workspace."

Model 3: A positive way of identifying the behavior in need of change is "I stay seated at all times. I remain in the assigned work area."

• *Problem:* Making noise (mumbling, grumbling, laughing, snorting, giggling, and so on)

Models 1 and 2: Issue a fine of $10/3 HF discs. In a neutral tone and manner, state, "There is a fine of $10 for making noise in this classroom" or "You are fined 3 HF discs for noisemaking."

Model 3: A positive way of identifying the problem behavior is "I will work on my assigned tasks quietly."

• *Problem:* Argumentative response

Models 1 and 2: Issue a fine of $15/4 HF discs. State, "Arguing is fined $15" or "Being argumentative with others in this group is fined 4 HF discs."

Model 3: A positive way of identifying the problem behavior is "I will listen to and follow the directions. I will raise my hand if I have questions about the directions."

• *Problem:* Off-task behavior (any behavior that interferes with or is inconsistent with the assigned task, e.g., daydreaming, playing with pencil, fidgeting, doodling)

Models 1 and 2: Issue a fine of $10/3 HF discs. State, "Off-task behavior is fined $10 (3 HF discs) in this group."

Model 3: A positive way of identifying the problem behavior is "I will attend to my assigned task in the manner expected and complete my work as directed."

DISCIPLINE AND CONTROL

No form of discipline should overlook or insult the child's self-worth and human dignity. This holds true especially for hyperactive children, for whom failure and criticism have become all too common and familiar.

When faced with unacceptable behavior, some teachers try to reason with the child. With the hyperactive child, however, this usually locks teacher and child into endless power struggles. Other teachers attempt to overlook problems, but we have found that overlooking a problem today invites recurrence tomorrow. Although setting and enforcing limits consistently is time-consuming at the outset, it pays off in the long run.

TIME OUT

Some people object to Time Out on the grounds that it is harsh, cruel, and an assault on the child's dignity. The purpose of Time Out, however, is not just to isolate the child (although it often gives the child a needed opportunity to calm down); its value lies in the withdrawal of attention and other positive consequences following misbehavior. When a child consistently violates limits, in spite of fines and other forms of negative feedback, a Time Out procedure should be used. Time Out is also an appropriate consequence for temper tantrums and aggressive behavior.

Time Out does not always require an extended period of time, but in order to be effective there must be absolutely no interaction with the child while he is in Time Out. This means that neither teacher nor peers should converse with the child nor respond to any bids for attention. In addition, all objects which are hazards or potential hazards should be removed from the area so that the child cannot harm himself or use the threat of self-harm to gain attention.

In the classroom, Time Out can be implemented in a variety of ways and does not necessarily involve physical removal or isolation. At the NIMH, we use Time Out as a four-stage process, described below. The least restrictive methods should be used first, with the more restrictive methods reserved for unsuccessful interventions and for physically aggressive behavior.

Initially, the use of Time Out may involve just withdrawing attention from the child. By actively attending to and praising classmates who are behaving appropriately, the teacher delivers a clear message about the kinds of behavior to which he or she will respond.

As a second step, materials and equipment should be taken away from the child and his activity interrupted. For example:

• If Tom is coloring the table instead of the paper, paper and crayons are removed for three minutes.

• If Tony is playing with the game materials instead of watching his opponent's moves, he loses his next turn.

• If Sean is playing with his pencil instead of working on his math, his pencil and book are removed for five minutes. If he fails to finish the assignment in the allotted time, he must make up the time after class.

When materials are removed, the child will often attempt to gain the teacher's attention with a temper tantrum or a verbal outburst. Fines should be imposed for this behavior. When the child has waited quietly and the designated time is up, materials should be returned.

Physical removal of the child from the group for the remaining period is the third stage. Because the child can only sit and watch during Time Out, he temporarily loses the reinforcement of being in the group and interacting with the others.

Finally, physical isolation in a secluded, unstimulating environment may be required. A partitioned corner, an empty closet, or a large appliance box can serve as an effective isolation area. Remove any articles that might prove hazardous to the child, such as belts, shoes, and jewelry. Send the child immediately to the Time Out area when an infraction occurs. Do not engage in discussion. If you argue with the child, you are giving him attention for his unacceptable behavior. The message of Time Out is, "Right now, your behavior is so unacceptable that no one wants to be with you. When you can express your feelings with words rather than actions, and when you are ready to work in the group, you may return." A period of five consecutive minutes of quiet behavior is enough in most cases.

Initially, when this system is implemented, you can expect frequent Time Outs and much testing of limits. This is the child's way of challenging the system. The extra time and effort necessary to apply the system consistently and firmly each and every time will ultimately be rewarded with a more cooperative child. Remember, things often get worse before they get better. Stick with the plan!

PREVENTIVE STRATEGIES

In the public school setting, it is not always easy to use physical isolation. In any case, it is far better to intervene early in a sequence of behavior to avert problems and avoid the need for Time Out. The following tactics help avoid the need for more restrictive measures:

   • *Acceptance and redirection of feelings.* When a child is frustrated, angry, or upset, teacher can help by accepting the child's feelings as valid while suggesting acceptable outlets for these feelings, such as "I know you're mad at Tim. Tell me in words why you are mad at him" or "I can see that you are very angry. You may hit the punching bag to get those feelings out. Then we can talk about it."

• *Guidance.* By giving a clue or a boost when a child is stuck, the teacher can help the hyperactive child solve his own problems without excessive frustration and humiliation: "These are like the problems you did yesterday. Do you remember how you did them?"

• *Signals.* Nonverbal signals, agreed upon by teacher and child, can be used to cue the child that his behavior is approaching out of bounds. Nonverbal cues show the teacher's concern and avoid attracting the attention of others in the class. This allows the child to exercise control and maintain his dignity.

• *Regrouping.* When a child becomes too frustrated to cope successfully with a task, transfer him to another meaningful but less taxing activity. He can experience success with this activity and return to the original task with renewed confidence.

• *Permission to throw a tantrum.* Giving the child permission to throw a tantrum, with the stipulation that he may not harm himself or others, can be useful when a child persistently denies that he is upset even though his actions clearly show that he is. Often the child will see no appeal in drawing this kind of attention to himself and will choose to discuss the problem instead.

Notes

1. Berry, C. A., S. E. Shaywitz, and B. A. Shaywitz. "Girls with Attention Deficit Disorder: A Silent Minority? A Report on Behavioral and Cognitive Characteristics." *Pediatrics,* 1985, vol. 76, p. 801.

2. Wender, P. H. *The Hyperactive Child, Adolescent, and Adult: Attention Deficit Disorder Through the Lifespan.* New York: Oxford University Press, 1987.

3. Ferber, R. *Solve Your Child's Sleep Problems.* New York: Simon and Schuster, 1985.

4. Breen, Michael. Personal communication, November 1987.

5. Ibid.

6. Wender, P. H. *Minimal Brain Dysfunction in Children.* New York: Wiley-Interscience, 1971.

7. Barkley, R. A. *Hyperactive Children: A Handbook for Diagnosis and Treatment.* New York: Guilford Press, 1981.

8. Chess, S., and A. Thomas. *Origins and Evolution of Behavior Disorders: From Infancy to Early Adult Life.* New York: Brunner/Mazel, 1984.

9. Hartsough, C. S., and N. M. Lambert. "Medical Factors in Hyperactive and Normal Children: Prenatal, Developmental, and Health History Findings." *American Journal of Orthopsychiatry,* 1985, vol. 55, p. 190.

10. Bellack, L. In *Attention Deficit Disorder: Diagnostic, Cognitive, and Thera-*

peutic Understanding, edited by L. M. Bloomingdale. New York: SP Medical and Scientific Books, 1984, p. 29.

11. Lou, H. C., L. Hendricksen, and P. Bruhn. "Focal Cerebral Hypoperfusion in Children with Dysphasia and/or Attention-deficit Disorder." *Archives of Neurology,* 1984, Volume 41, p. 825.

12. Bradley, C. "The Behavior of Children Receiving Benzedrine." *American Journal of Psychiatry,* 1937, Volume 94, p. 577.

13. Klein, D. F., R. Gittelman, F. Quitkin, and A. Rifkin. *Diagnosis and Drug Treatment of Psychiatric Disorders: Adults and Children,* 2nd ed. Baltimore: Williams and Wilkins, 1980.

14. Chatoor, I., K. Wells, C. K. Conners, W. Seidel, and D. Shaw. "The Effects of Nocturnally Administered Stimulant Medication on EEG Sleep and Behavior in Hyperactive Children." *Journal of the American Academy of Child Psychiatry,* 1983, vol. 22, p. 337.

15. Wender, P. H. *The Hyperactive Child.*

16. Dulcan, M. K. "The Psychopharmacologic Treatment of Children and Adolescents with Attention Deficit Disorder." *Psychiatric Annals,* 1985, vol. 15, p. 69.

17. Weiss, G., and L. T. Hechtman. *Hyperactive Children Grown Up.* New York: Guilford Press, 1986.

18. Sleator, E. K., R. K. Ullman, and A. von Neumann. "How Do Hyperactive Children Feel About Taking Stimulants and Will They Tell the Doctor?" *Clinical Pediatrics,* 1982, vol. 21, p. 474.

19. Rancurello, M. D. "Clinical Applications of Antidepressant Drugs in Childhood Behavioral and Emotional Disorders." *Psychiatric Annals,* 1985, vol. 15, p. 88.

20. Wender, P. H., D. R. Wood, F. W. Reimherr, and M. Ward. "An Open Trial of Pargyline in the Treatment of Attention Deficit Disorder, Residual Type." *Psychiatry Research,* 1983, vol. 9, p. 329.

21. Milich, R., M. Wolraich, and S. Lindgren. "Sugar and Hyperactivity: A Critical Review of Empirical Findings." *Clinical Psychology Review,* 1986, vol. 6, p. 493.

22. Wender, P. H. *Minimal Brain Dysfunction in Children.*

23. Douglas, V. I. "Are Drugs Enough? To Treat or Train the Hyperactive Child." In *Recent Advances in Child Psychopharmacology,* edited by R. Gittelman-Klein. New York: Human Sciences Press, 1975, p. 203.

24. Brown, R. T., M. E. Wynne, and R. Medenis. "Methylphenidate and Cognitive Therapy: A Comparison of Treatment Approaches with Hyperactive Boys." *Journal of Abnormal Child Psychology,* 1985, vol. 13, p. 1063.

25. Abikoff, H., and R. Gittelman. "Hyperactive Children Treated with Stimulants." *Archives of General Psychiatry,* 1985, vol. 42, p. 953.

26. *Ibid.*

27. Arnold, L. E. "Parents of Hyperactive and Aggressive Children." In *Helping Parents Help Their Children*, edited by L. E. Arnold. New York: Brunner/Mazel, 1978, p. 193.

28. Taylor, J. F. *The Hyperactive Child and the Family*. New York: Dodd, Mead, 1980.

29. *Ibid.*

30. Smith, S. L. *No Easy Answers: The Learning Disabled Child at Home and at School*. New York: Winthrop, 1979.

31. Rohrkemper, M. "Individual Differences in Students' Perceptions of Routine Classroom Events." *Journal of Educational Psychology*, 1985, vol. 77, p. 29.

32. Smith, S. L. *No Easy Answers*.

33. *Ibid.*

34. Rapport, M., A. Murphy, and J. S. Bailey. "The Effects of a Response Cost Treatment Tactic on Hyperactive Children." *Journal of School Psychology*, 1980, vol. 18, p. 98.

35. Barclay, J. R. "Effecting Behavior Change in the Elementary Classroom: An Exploratory Study." *Journal of Counseling Psychology*, 1967, vol. 14, p. 240.

36. Gittelman, R. "Treatment of Reading Disorders." In *Developmental Neuropsychiatry*, edited by M. Rutter. New York: Guilford Press, 1983, p. 520.

37. Glynn, E. L., and J. D. Thomas. "Effect of Cueing on Self-Control of Classroom Behavior." *Journal of Applied Behavior Analysis*, 1974, vol. 7, p. 299.

Index

Barbara Ingersoll has treated hyperactive children and counseled their families for eighteen years. She holds a Ph.D. in clinical psychology from Pennsylvania State University. She has been an Associate Professor at West Virginia University Medical School and is now on the clinical faculty in their Department of Behavioral Medicine and Psychiatry. She lives in Bethesda, Maryland.